IMAGES OF IRELAND

LISMORE

IMAGES OF IRELAND

LISMORE

EUGENE F. DENNIS

NONSUCH

First published 2005
Reprinted 2005

Nonsuch Publishing Limited
73 Lower Leeson Street
Dublin 2
Ireland

www.nonsuchireland.com

National Library Cataloguing in Publication Data.
A catalogue record for this book is available from the National Library.

ISBN 1-84588-501-5

Typesetting and origination by Tempus Publishing Limited.
Printed in Great Britain.

Contents

Acknowledgements

Those who helped with the project are sincerely thanked, especially the heroic Paddy Vaughan, Tommy Keating and James Lenane, James coming on board at an appropriate point to help lay down a preliminary template. That 'greatest' Lismoreian Ned Barry, who sadly died in February 2005, must get a thousand thanks for help and advice and a hundred thanks to Seán Doocey, Walter Barry, Tony Dowd and a number of friends in Lismore and Cork who helped keep the project afloat at a critical stage. The GAA and the Hotel were also very accommodating. Pauline Ryan (sacristan) is commended for offering prompt display of notices, as are many shops. Thanks are due to The Dungarvan Leader, The Dungarvan Observer, The Avondhu, and Irish Examiner Publications. Ballysaggart GAA Remembers 1984 and Ireland: Photographs 1840-1930, compiled by Seán Sexton, Laurence King, 1994, were two useful sources. Also, a word of gratitude is owed to the many anonymous photographers down the years.

The public is offered a míle buíochas (a thousand thanks) for their donations and information. Photographs are of great sentimental value to people: to hand them over to anyone involves a fine mutual trust. Project SMILE, the name given to the overall initiative to collect old Lismore Photographs, is grateful for the widespread trust placed in it. The author set up project SMILE in 2003 to collect and publish a book of old Lismore photos, old meaning, up to the late-1960s with a few exceptions. Photographs were first taken in Ireland in about 1840, very shortly after Monsieur Daguerre invented the process. Lismore was lucky in having Francis Edmund Currey who had a studio in the Castle in the late 1840s. After Currey, it was all downhill, and hence the tradition is a fragmented one.

The photographic heritage is very fragile: a place of Lismore's size loses one old photograph a week. Photography is a crucial aspect of heritage because photographs remember, people forget. In the press release for SMILE, it was jokingly suggested that there might be more promise of immortality in photography than in religion. The readying of a collection of old photos is demanding, especially if one wants to access what may be called 'the people's photos'. These are not readily available like the work of pioneers like Currey and Lawrence; they are part in truth of the hidden and often inaccessible Ireland.

Each and every photograph not only tells it own story but also has its own mini biography, for example, a photo of one premises required examining the deeds involved to establish its provenance. Selecting is a happy headache, but competition must be between photos based on vintage, quality, rarity, etc. The author takes responsibility for any errors occurring in the text. Overall the project was both frustrating and challenging, even surprisingly so, but in the end one hopes it was worthwhile.

The Lismore Crozier and Boss

The Lismore Crozier was found, along with the Book of Lismore, in 1814 in a blocked doorway in Lismore Castle. The Crozier, which is forty inches in length, is one of the few surviving masterpieces of early Irish Christian art. It is made of metal – a pale bronze covered with richly gilded ornaments and animal heads and set with enamels. The drop of the crook originally contained a reliquary or shrine for relics. Two lines at the base of the crook record the name of Neachtan, the craftsman and of the client, Niall Mac Mhic Aodhagain, Bishop of Lismore 1090-1113. The Crozier is housed in the National Museum in Dublin.

Introduction

Lismore: A Brief History

The origins of Lismore are entangled in legend and problematic history. Legends are best let lie since they often do, which isn't to deny their charm, for example, Lismore being named by a holy woman who met St Carthage on his arrival to found his monastery in the seventh century. The motto on the ancient arms of Lismore, 'God's providence is our inheritance', betrays ecclesiastic origins, but the older names Dúnsginne, Magh na Sciath and Lismore itself betray defensive origins (Dún and Lios are forts while Sciath is a shield). Whatever the case, Lismore is renowned as the site of a famous double monastery, which had twenty churches at its height and was a University city. It attracted such luminaries as St Cadoc of Wales, St Cathaldus of Tarentum and Alfred the Great of 'the burnt cakes'. A Lismore boast goes: when Oxford was a cowpath Lismore was a flourishing University city!

Lismore's renown must have been great because it was the first monastery – then the equivalent of a settlement – to be sacked by the Vikings and repeatedly so. Against the odds, Lismore survived and was a stronghold of reform and the céle Dé (culdee) or anchorite movement. This latter was very strict, but creative in art and music, for example, the making of the processional Lismore Crozier and the likely composing of the hymn 'Be Thou My Vision' in Lismore. In about 1120 Lismore became the See of the Decies diocese.

Soon after King Henry II arrived in Ireland, he went to Lismore in furtherance of his imperial pretensions. There he met the Bishop of Lismore who was also the Papal Legate and Munster chiefs at a synod-council type meeting. Henry was granted a Charter to the sovereignty of Ireland in perpetuity. Thus it was that Lismore was where English Law was first promulgated in Ireland – to paraphrase the town motto, 'Henry's Lismore Charter was Ireland's inheritance'. Henry also chose the site for a castle, which Prince John built. This castle in time became the Episcopal residence – a bishop then being a kind of super civil servant with diverse secular duties. Bishop Myler McGrath sold the castle to Sir Walter Raleigh; he then sold it to Richard Boyle. In 1753, the Castle and estates passed to the Fourth Duke of Devonshire on his marriage to Lady Charlotte Boyle.

The Castle, as we now know it, was designed by Joseph Paxton for the Sixth, or Bachelor Duke. These two men are key to Lismore's basic plan and layout. The Convent too was designed by Paxton and Botany laid out in the 1820s. In 1824 R.H. Ryland wrote the following: 'Lismore is now a thriving town, and, if we may judge by the spirit of building which prevails, and from the many new streets now in progress, the trade and wealth of the inhabitants are increasing.'

Places have phases – Lismore, once an inviolable Episcopal city, then a ducal appendage, and now Ireland's 'Tidiest Town' (won in September 2004). Though pride be a vice, there is a pride allied to virtue – the pride of a place in its history, people and tradition. Lismoreians can certainly indulge that. This book should be a small contribution to illuminating the object of pride and hence, perhaps increasing it. The work cannot be definitive, as the subject matter is infinite, but let the photographs speak for themselves, as the image is mightier than the pen.

Eugene Dennis
August 2004

Eugene Dennis
A biographical note

Eugene Dennis became a freelance journalist having taught for many years. He broadcast many *Sunday Miscellany* scripts in the 1980s. Along with editorial work, he has written three educational monographs and published two well-received poetry collections. A collection of short stories, *Look Back and Wonder* is due out later in 2005. He lives in Cork.

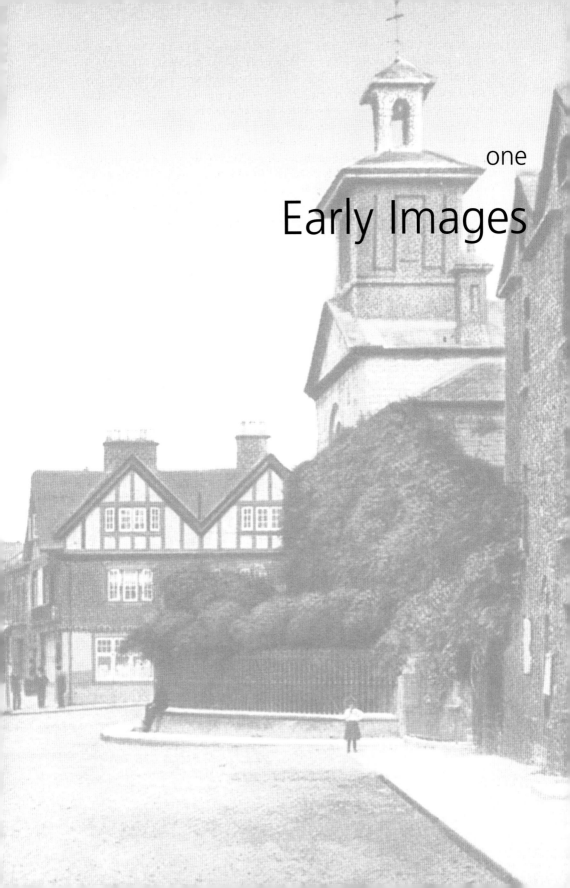

one

Early Images

Head Constable Kieley and the egg woman around 1853. The old woman selling surplus farm produce from door to door, on the streets or in the local market gazes blankly at the camera. Documentary photography was rare at this stage and this is very likely her first time to see such a device and she may well fear it. The photograph is from the Francis Edmund Currey collection.

The Red House taking shape in a massive makeover around 1903, and the locals could sit 'squarely round the Monument' for a chat. The advance party for King Edward VII's visit of May 1904 found the accommodation for his entourage rather inadequate, hence The Red House was in receipt of an upgrade. It was at the time quite a rather modest inn, described as a dilapidated 'shebeen' by one critic. Investigations revealed that the Red House was so named in 1904.

The old railway bridge in Lismore is now but a memory. Through the eye of the bridge the town's park is clearly visible with no dwellings in sight. The three children seem splendid in appearance and attire; two carrying what look like early ponchos! The young buck is surely bringing a skillet or pot-pan 'for the smithie to be a fixin'.

Repairing Lismore Bridge after flood damage of 1853. This snap too, is a fine example of Currey's documentary skill. This photo, with a number of others, has only recently come to light. Kind permission was granted by Lismore Estates to use the photograph along with the 'The Guard' on page 13 for the first time.

We'd like to think there's whiskey in that jar! The precise provenance of this photograph is somewhat unclear. The building could be a farm one or a merchant's storehouse for grain. The strings or 'yorks' on the man's trousers were used where rats were a danger. An exclusive capturing of Lismoreians nearly a century ago. It is likely the whiskey or porter jar is what is evoking the suggestion of a smile and not the camera.

Opposite below: Chapel Street at a time when people were more street-frequenting than they are now. The telegraphic lines are visible on the left and the gas lamps, on the right. The bulky bags aboard the carts are very likely full of wool going to a market. The photograph was taken nearly a century ago and this is the first time being published. The four recessed houses, obscured by wool carts, were just built by Larry Fitzgerald. This space was previously partially filled by two thatched houses.

Above: 'The Guard' at Lismore Castle around 1854. A formidable group of soldiery or redcoats readying up for some unknown assignment.

A beautiful Lady of Ballinwillin. Ellen Lyons was born around a decade after the Great Famine. Marrying John O'Donnell, she had ten children – one of whom was called Tommy 'The Master' O'Donnell of great local renown and Mary Anne O'Donnell, who became the mother of Mick and Tim Doherty of Lismore. This portrait of Ellen was taken around 1928 and is still displayed in Mick Doherty's home. The mystery and fetch of this image is timeless.

'Dunney and his Dudeen'. A splendid portrait of a self-reliant earthy man with what is probably a home-made or clay pipe. He is Patrick Dunne, great-grandfather of the children of Liam and Pauline Ryan (née Dunne) from Bóthar Mochuda. He is buried in the Catholic section of the Church of Ireland.

An ivied Lismore Castle. Built initially by Henry II and Prince John, it eventually fell to the Bishops of Lismore. The apostate Myler McGrath sold it to Sir Walter Raleigh, he to Boyle and then finally on to the titled Cavendish family, which makes it still a ducal residence. The design is composite, not excluding Irish Romanesque and King John's Tower too, simulates the Irish Round Tower. A gem as Castles go; its recent illumination renders it altogether magical.

By now an immemorial view of Main Street around 1904. Note the good standard surfacing and paving with the exception perhaps of some work in progress in foreground left.

A medieval concept of Lismore as captured by artist Uto Hogerzeil. In a sense the camera was a spoilsport, as it freed art from the need to be representational. Welles showed in *Citizen Kane* you could photograph an idea but only an artist could summon this impressionistic 'concept' of Lismore.

The Church of Ireland Cathedral as captured by the architect McIvory. The headstones, rising ground in background and trees betray an early impressionistic touch. The Cathedral that we now know is inviting perhaps even prettified. This image suggests a little the remoteness of God even if moderated by open door accessibility. A Cathedral, nevertheless, that combines a murkiness (its bishop murdered on the site) and apostasy (from catholic to protestant in the seventeenth century) with a glorious history.

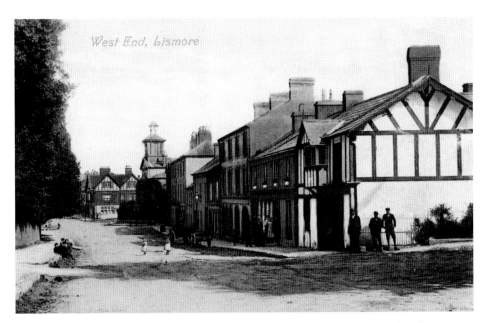

A view of West Street in the early twentieth century. This street was developed in the 1850s and is today very much a business street. The street leads on to Gallows Hill of evil memory, which at the top is dominated by the old Christian Brothers' Monastery (now County Council offices and library). On the right going up, is the old Carnegie Library designed by George Sheridan in the hiberno-romanesque style.

The ivied Town Hall. This striking building has served many purposes and has had different names such as Court House and now the Heritage Centre. This view is a century old. This is an edifice that always successfully reinvents itself, even after the disastrous fire of 1920 – as a later picture shows.

The Presentation Convent, Lismore was founded in 1836. Four sisters established themselves in the North Mall. By 1840 the sisters had their convent on stream designed by Sir Joseph Paxton, later architect of the Crystal Palace in London. In the famine years, the nuns introduced lace-making and knitting industries. In 1925 the Maher Memorial secondary school was opened on the site of an old Protestant school. In 1946, a new primary school was opened. By the 1980s, vocations were drying up and in 1991, it was announced that the nuns were leaving Lismore. In this early view of the Convent we can see St Bruno's Hall to the left.

Lismore from Ballygallane, 1746

The dedication on this prospect is by Charles Smith, the noted historian of counties Waterford, Cork and Kerry and whom Canon Power D. Litt claimed lived in Lismore working as an apothecary or a doctor.

Opposite above: The Butter Factory was a kind of palace of dreams of butter making and was owned by Arthur Paxman, at the canal-warehousing site in Ballyrafter. The butter was bought at markets roundabout in an unsalted state and then processed for wider distribution. There were also poultry and box-making sections in the factory.

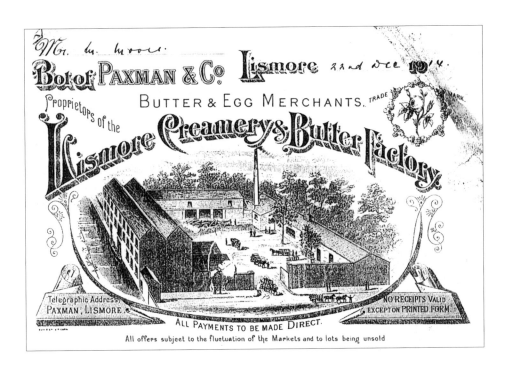

Above: Currey's Garden. The walled-in garden was in Lower Church Lane between the houses and the Warren. The photograph was taken around 1918 – the first on the left at the back being M. Behegan, who emigrated to the USA, fourth left may be Mr Currey, sixth from the left is Mike Parker, while third from the left in front may be Mrs Currey. The workers are harvesting daffodil bulbs for export, the seed having been sown in September. The plough harnessed to the jennet or mule is a Cooke No. 2 and is kept now as a relic by a local farmer. Others who worked in the garden were 'Cuddy' Power, Mattie Kavanagh (later MBE), Mary O'Callaghan (New Street) and Mr O'Sullivan (grandfather of Seán Mayfield).

'Mick-the-Bird', or Mick O'Brien of Botany – A character in his time and a man of boundless old world charm and amiability. The Father of Pad, 'the Drummer', who succeeded him at the Wine Vaults, 'Mick-the-Post', Nell Foley and Kit Neville, andalso Chris, Harry and Joan who emigrated.

Opposite above: This fine portrait was taken around 1910. From left to right: Joe O'Donnell, John Hickey, Andy Hickey – proprietor, the Hickey sisters Annie and Mary, Seamus Ryan (of Church Lane), Jack Bennett (with bike) and Tom Curran. Andy also had an early garage nearby. Peadar, his son, later ran it and a hackney service. Note the thatched roof where the garage was; it is still a garage under the proprietorship of Maurice Dunne.

Opposite below: Lady Louise's Bridge over the Owennashad was a beautiful accommodation bridge that led to the seventy-two steps, woodland and the quarry. It was still crossable in the 1940s, but by the next decade it had virtually disappeared.

Above: The Workhouse, Poorhouse or Union. The Workhouse was opened in 1814 for the dispossessed. A house of last resort where arbitrary rule reigned. Suppliants were hunger-driven; their life-thirst often consumed by ring of hell-fever and shame. On one day alone, thirteen wan cadavers were relayed in a circulating coffin to the graveyard. The Mercy nuns tried hard as did personnel but economics defeats charity. Redeemed later as a District Hospital and Sanatorium, it closed in the 1990s.

Below: The focus in this photo, taken about a century ago, is on both the Devonshire Arms Hotel and the Monument. Note the Hotel's partially covered ivy frontage. The Hotel opened for business in the late 1880s after it was built as an adjunct to Castle accommodation as the first purpose-built hotel in Ireland. It has had such notables guests as Major Henry Eeles – the scientist who is buried on Knockmealdown Mountain ('in the erect position upside down', it is said), also Thackeray – author of Vanity Fair, and in recent times, Jeremy Paxman, who is connected to Paxman's of Lismore Butter Factory fame. The Monument, a gothic fountain, was erect in 1872 in honour of Archdeacon Ambrose Power.

Above and below: Two views of New Street or 'Botany' taken some time in mid-twentieth century. The photograph above is of Upper- or Top-Botany. The scene captures a time of transition in vehicular traffic as, apart from the car, we see a cart in the background. The car's owner was Jimmy 'The Hawk' O'Brien, who had a hackney service and the cart, is Flynn's. Noteworthy too, is the single canopy in contrast to the view in Lower Botany in the photo below. Here Sheila Fenton stands at her door, perhaps wondering where her dog Rex was – it was actually the dog in the Top Botany photo! The donkey and cart is Ned Barry's and the woman crossing the street is thought to be Bina Devine.

All the canopies are now removed bar one. Botany was laid out around 1820 by the Sixth Duke for the Estate's tenants and was dubbed Botany by residents because they felt removed as far as Botany Bay from their old homes near the Castle.

Lismore decorated for King Edward VII's visit in May 1904. Closer scrutiny of the image will reveal scaffolding in front of the current Castle Lodge Bar and Restaurant. The decorator, Dick Willoughby, declined the request to remove the scaffold. In Dick's thinking, work should go on, King or no king

two

Work and Living

This portrait of the O'Farrell family of Ashbourne Townspark was taken in 1904. From left to right, back row: Dick O'Farrell, Fr O'Farrell (Frogmore, Youghal), May O'Farrell, Mrs Margaret O'Farrell, Tess O'Farrell and Fr Michael O'Farrell, who ministered in New York, especially to Irish immigrants. He co-founded the College of New Rochelle and became its first president. He celebrated Mass in Lismore in 1884 in the newly restored St Carthage's Cathedral. Front row: Paddy O' Farrell, Hannah O' Farrell, Michael Carthage O'Farrell, Shaun O'Farrell, James O'Farrell, John O'Farrell and Elizabeth O'Farrell.

This group was taken at Sheehan's seat on West Street around 1960. Only the men in the photograph are Lismoreians. From left to right: Jim Ahearne ('Slog'), Tommy Kearney (Tourin-Botany), Mick Stapleton ('Stork-een'), Johnny Stapleton ('Fopper') and Pat Neville (extreme right). The ladies and youngsters were day-trippers to Lismore.

John and Betty Scanlan, Main Street, Lismore 'taking the water' in Mount Melleray in 1932. This water feature was by the College. Both the College and the water feature are now gone. All of the Scanlans emigrated. Their old newspaper shop lies vacant; Breeda Carroll (Scanlan) sadly reflecting that it would go back to the laneway it was once, leading to the Catholic Cathedral.

Bravery award being made to fearless Lismore fire fighter Stephen (Steve) Kennefick in June 2000. From left to right: ACFO Billy Hickey, SO Eric Flynn, SUBO Con MacNamara, CFO Tony McCarthy, SS Seán Sheehan, Stephen 'Hero' Kennefick, Dr FF Martin Landers, ACFO Des O'Brien and FF Mary McNamara.

FRIENDS OF LISMORE HANDBALL ALLEY

'Handball....
The Liveliest Game'

'Cluiche na nDaoine'

*'Serving balls
for over a 100 years'*

You indifferent, buck your courage
You alley lovers, fight
Stand Lismore for your heritage
Pray for the philistines: do the right

An Coiste Ad Hoc, Eanáir 2004

CAIRDE DE CHÚIRT LIATHRÓID LÁIMHE, LIOS MÓR

The ball alley in Church Lane is now an antiquity (100 years old). Built as a gesture of defiance, it was once a mecca and is still a useful playing space, whose real purpose may revive. It is now a listed or protected building.

Above left: Eva and Michael 'Silversides' O'Neill around 1960. This couple lived in East Main Street. Michael was a talented gardener and Eva (née Wright) taught at the Convent.

Above right: Patrick and Mary O'Farrell of Cooldelane, Lismore in 1948. This portrait was taken on the occasion of their daughter Aileen's first visit home from USA. The portrait may show, as Bob Hope said, 'that fashion is something that goes in one era and out the other'.

A view of what later became known as the Commercial Hotel in the South Mall, this shot dates from 1889. The lady holding the baby is Ellen O'Donnell (née Canty) and the baby is thought to be Frank O'Donnell. Pat Hale and his wife ran the hotel in the early days and then their relations the O'Donnells ran it, John O'Donnell having returned from South Africa. The hotel has served Lismore in a quiet but efficient way over decades.

This features the six Doocey boys and their mum at Deerpark in 1956. From left to right: Tony, Willie, Noel, Dick, Tom, Seán and Mrs Madge Doocey.

Lismore Agricultural Show June 1929. Four students of Melleray College proudly display their shorthorn (rowan and black) prize winners in a stock-judging competition. A very talented Lismore (Glencairn) man headed the Agricultural Department at Melleray at this time namely, Paddy Heskin (brother of Denis and George) – then a monk at Melleray.

Above left: An image of a medal won at Lismore Agriculture Show in 1884. The medal was awarded to Mr Parker of Roseville Tallow (now O'Keeffe's), for the best pen of aged-ewes. The medal is a splendid specimen, both for its size and design.

Above right: Scuffling Spuds in Bishopstown in 1955. Tom and Joan Hennessy scuffling the potatoes with the crucial help of Neddy. A little bit of compulsive, if not compulsory tillage! As Paddy Barry of Ballyin used to say: 'after tillage, other arts follow'. And yes, the weather was always perfect in those days!

Billhead of John O'Brien's garage from 1918 – arguably the first garage in Lismore. The O'Briens were a famous family of artisans, but the garage business declined as the family diversified into the building-decorating business.

Group photograph taken on the occasion of the West Waterford Hunt Club's annual ball in Lismore Castle, January 1930. Included at the back are: Senator John Keane, Mrs Baring, Mrs Percy Smyth, Mrs Masters, Perceval Maxwell, E. Rohan and T.C. Williams. Front row, Sir Ernest Goff, Lady Musgrave, Sir Thomas Ainsworth, MFH, Dorothy Musgrave, MFH (West Waterford's), Hon. Claud Anson, Lady Ainsworth and Lady Patricia Miller.

Ellen (Nellie) Murphy and her brothers Edward and Michael around 1896. The Murphys farmed in Okyle. Edward subsequently set up a successful drapery business in West End, Lismore.

This shot was taken in 1963. Bob and Daisy Allison the owners of the drapery stand near the entrance. The shop was opened by Bob in 1934, Bob being considered a formidable draper. Three assistants who worked with him were Michael Broderick (Br Aengus), Norah O'Gorman and the once fine ragtrade man, Tom Noonan. It is now the Lismore Bookshop, under the proprietorship of James Hyde. The Allison's shop-front is typical of the traditional shop-fronts dating from Parnellite times. Fortunately many of these shop-fronts still exist and one, the Mall Bar was recently granted protected building status.

Above: Ballinvella ICA Group around 1962. The ICA (Irish Countrywomen's Association) was set up in Lismore in 1959, having been founded in Wexford in 1910 by Anita Letts. The ICA, is like the WI (Women's Institute) in the UK. A wonderful organisation, it promotes the arts and crafts and supports most community endeavours, be they cultural, educational or humanitarian. The photograph includes from left to right: Pauline O'Donnell (Camphire), Mrs Schiller, Mary Hickey (née Tobin), Nell Mangan, Norah Dunne and Lucy Collender.

Previous page below: This photograph was taken at Bill Canning's (Monatrim) eighty-fifth birthday in Ashford, Co Wicklow. From left to right: Charlie Brady, Brian Pearce and Bill Canning. Charlie Brady, a still life and landscape painter, was a New Yorker who came to Lismore in 1956. He met and later married Eelagh Noonan. Brady cut out a distinct niche in Irish painting for himself, completing small-scale still lifes like bus tickets, pegs, torn envelopes or even detritus. He won the Douglas Hyde gold medal twice, a recognition of his true painting finesse. He died in 1997. Brady painted some fine scenes around Lismore, as did his brother-in-law, John Noonan in the 1950s. Brian Pearce was a leading farmer in West Waterford and founder member of the old National Farmers' Association.

Left: This fountain graced the centre of the showgrounds or Fair Field at one time. Though not particularly handsome, it wasn't without charm. It still exists and if battered, it could be restored. The boy on second left is Richie Cahill; the others on holiday from Galway.

Tom Hickey (left) and George McDonagh, with the prize for a raffle at a dance in Hartington Hall in 1926. The prize was a badger mounted on a stand. The price for admission to the dance was two shillings. Both men went on to fame, Tom as a journalist, George as a businessman.

John Mangan, off to the fair in the late 1930s with a 'beautiful bulbous mass of baskets'. John was known as 'The Champ' for his brilliant skill at basket making. Josie and Nell Mangan also had rare skill – the latter two in lace-making, and they taught that intricate skill in An Grianán, home of the Irish Countrywomen's Association.

Threshing at Jerry O'Brien's Monamom in September 1949. From left to right: Tom Doocey, Paddy Doocey, Billy Mulcahy (Church Lane) and Ger Fraher. The photograph was taken by Jim O'Brien who was on holidays from New York. The threshing machine belonged to J.F. O'Donnell, one of the famous Blackwater Ramblers of his day.

Above: Pad O'Brien (son of 'Mick-the-Bird', an earlier driver) at the reins of McCarthy's delivery-cart in November 1951. Pad delivered to hinterlands such as Strancally, Tourin and Ballinvella. Pad himself was a highly regarded gentleman and fine bandsman, both in the army and in civilian life.

Left: An early bicycle shop in West Street from 1910. Bets Daly lives in this house now. On the left is Con O'Neill and in the middle John O'Neill, close relatives of the Willoughby family. The youth's name is not known.

Partying at the Castle around 1950s. Among those standing from left are: Billy King (fourth left), Mr Silcock (eleventh left), Lord Hartington (thirteenth left), John Tobin (eighteenth left), Kate O'Connell (nineteenth left), Bertie Neville (second right), Mrs Crowley (third right) and Mrs Hickey (fourth right). Sitting from left to right: Mrs Scanlan, Mrs Mullins, Mrs Feeney, John 'Parrot' O'Doherty (fifth left), Mary Feeney (sixth adult on left),Garret Hogan (seventh left),Tom Hale (ninth 1eft) Norrie O'Riordan (second right) and Kathleen Hogan (née Crowley, extreme right).

Lismore Ladies Show Committee on 5 July 1950. From left to right: Mary Fives, Show Judge, Mary Willoughby, Madge Doocey, Nancy Cronin (Armstrong), Nellie O'Sullivan, Mary Doocey (Geary), Dorothea Daly (Lee), Bella Ellis, Mrs Hobson, Show Judge, Babs Canning and Show Judge.

Above: This picture is a rare and partial view of the Fever Hospital in the 1930s. This hospital was at the corner of the Boreen (Bóithrín) and Townspark. A hospital that suffered 'murcha' and was once used as a school. It was demolished around 1940. Oddly, Robert Armstrong's drawing of 1842 does not accord with its image here. Mrs O'Regan (grandmother of Joe) is seen at her door.

Left: This photograph was taken in 1938 and is, too, rare. It is Campion's bread delivery van, the only donkey or 'jennet-powered' one locally. The two aboard are Johnny Whelan and Bernie Feeney.

A devastating scene on Main Street, Lismore in 1940 after a disastrous fire gutted O'Connor's (Curtin's) butcher shop. Local volunteer fire-fighters were heroic on the night, including George O'Brien, still alive and well in the UK, (indeed George proved especially deft coming from the back roof to open the fire break down by the barge, hence stopping fire-spread to Moore's). For assurance help also arrived from Cork. Caught by the photographer was, on the left, Jimmy Fenton (Ferry Lane), Guard Purcell and a young Jim Campion may have been incautiously caught. Luckily there were no fire casualties but Jim Barry fell into the cellar and Jim McNamara jumped out a window onto a greenhouse and had to be hospitalised.

Lismore Macra na Feirme win Stock-Judging Cup in Cork around 1955. From left to right, back row: Eily O'Donnell, Bill Kennefick and Babs Canning. Front row: Michael O'Gorman, Dick Doocey and Liam (Bill) Ryan. Liam Ryan was, in particular, an outstanding judge of stock, winning an international competition in his heyday. This competition took place at Buckley's of Ballinahina on a 'Field Day' at the farm.

John Coleman's shop on Main Street was opened in 1926 as a general store, later it became a grain and milk store. This snapshot was taken in 1936. The young rascal messing in front is Mikey Coleman, later the non-pareil Fr Mikey himself, who is Japan-domiciled now for nearly half a century.

Bill 'The Comm' Power of Shrough is cutting hay with horses and a mowing machine in the 1940s. The scene is redolent of a more pastoral Ireland, 'The Comm' (from Commandent, a unique Irish Army title) is in direct and immediate control. A crucial task every year was saving the hay and then beating (in hurling) Cappoquin, the real old enemy.

Portrait of the Murphy family (Drapery) West Street around 1900. From left to right: Michael Murphy (accountant to Joseph McGrath of bloodstock-sweepstake notoriety), Mrs Murphy, Josie Murphy, Ellen (Nellie) Murphy (herself a teacher, she married an Eton master in the UK) and Edward Murphy (owner of the drapery).

A shot from the 1970s of one of the last public water taps in Lismore. It was sited in Church Lane where here two local women pose for the camera namely Nellie Ahern (on the left) and Betty Doherty.

Left: Three makeover experts snapped in June 1932. From left to right: Mick Power, Ned Nugent (lived then next to Babe Tierney's) and Tom Keating. Tom Keating was both an ordinary mason and a stone mason, the Keating family being formidable practitioners of the great stone cutting art. Tom also had his own band and hated the popular music then beginning to waft in. He also loved circuses and took a day off work when they came to town.

Below: Threshing at Doocey's Deerpark 1948. From left to right: Seán Barry, John Joe O'Donnell, Mike Corbett, Mike Baldwin, Bill Regan, 'Dame' James Heskin. In foreground Paddy Doocey smoking to heart's discontent! This photograph was taken by Miss Rice of South Mall Lismore.

A group of Jack Nugent's men building Fr Tom Murphy's kitchen in 1955. From left to right: John Bennett, Dan Shanahan (to front), Chris Foley (at Dan's shoulder), John Kennefick, Jimmy Sargent (Ballysaggart), Mick Foley (Ballyduff), Jimmy Arrigan (Cappoquin), Paddy Arrigan, William 'Marsh' Hickey.

Above: Members of the Lismore Agricultural Show Committee of 1947-1948, photographed at the Ellis home, now the home of the Twomeys. From left to right, back row: Der O'Donnell (Killahala), Harry Loftus (Dromana) and Jack Fives. Middle row: Paddy Barry (Glencairn), Tom Fives, John O'Donnell (Deerpark), Bella Ellis, Dave Barry (Glencairn), Matt Dromey (Dungarvarn), John 'Guyler' Greehy and Dave Walsh B. Ag. Sci. Seated: Alec Ellis and Mick Neill. On ground: the Neill brothers.

Opposite below: Lismore and Cappoquin Credit Union at Opening of Chapel Street Office, 1976. From left to right: John Ryan, Tony Bolger, Barry Daynes, Seán Jefferies, Rose Campion, Moss Pollard, Paddy Lawton, Helen Moore, Jackie Green, Tom Doocey, Paddy Pollard, Dermot O'Leary, Frank Geoghegan and Richard Brennan. Lismore Credit Union opened first day on 20 March 1971 in East Main Street, next to Dunne's garage until in 1973 it combined with Cappoquin. In 1990 the C. U. moved to Main Street. Its membership is now nearing 4,000, with shares totalling eight million Euro and a similar loan total.

Right: A stylish Bridie Coughlan stepping it out in Church Lane in the late 1950s. Note the portico, which was a fine feature of houses in Lower Church Lane. George (Seoirse) O'Brien has written wistfully of the Lane in his *The Village of Longing.*

Below: The Arcade in the late 1930s. From left to right: Sally Murphy (Nugent), Martin Healy (proprietor), Eily Healy (McCarthy) and Nellie O'Gorman (Hale). The Arcade closed down in recent times; it awaits a renaissance.

Portrait of Lismore's most multi-talented family, the O'Connors of Townspark at Goat Island Ardmore around 1949. From left to right, back row: Eddie and Michael J. Front row: Jimmy, Noel, Pat, Mrs Peg O'Connor, Rena and Ann. Eddie is a fine painter, Jimmy had great unrealized football talent, Pat is an award-winning film director, Noel an all-rounder, Rena a songwriter and Ann lead singer with the Bards.

Fear an Phoist and two lesser mortals! From left to right: Jim O'Donnell, Maureen Power (née Russell) and Seamus O'Donnell. Jim O'Donnell was Town Postman in the middle of the last century. His work he saw as a partnership with his bike. They were on talking terms and agreed on one thing- the post must go through!

Right: 'Exiles from Erin'. At back, John Crotty (Cappoquin). From left to right, front row: Mick Feeney, Ned Keyes, Pad Keyes. These men were working in the coalmines in Staffordshire just after the Second World War. They were recruited from the Labour Exchange to work on farms, mines and so on.

Below: Workers at the Nicotine Factory around 1930. This factory was located in 'The Hall', (later an army barracks in the Second World War and now Dowd's business) and run by Stuarts. The factory processed nicotine from tobacco, the product used to make sprays and assorted chemicals. It closed at the end of the 1930s. From left to right, back row: Tommy Uniacke, Paddy Hickey (Deerpark), Mick Power and John 'Jocklin' O'Donnell. The two in front are unknown.

The Mangans – Mr Jack Mangan in middle and sons John (left) and Denis – basket-making in Bridane Cottage in 1933. Up to about 1920 nearly every townland had craftsmen (mostly men) producing scibs or ciseáins (baskets) from sally rods. The Mangans, as did the Quinlans in Tallow, famously stayed with the craft and made a living from it. They extended their products over time to include garden seats, chairs, etc., and selling not only to the Irish but the UK market as well.

John O'Brien of Chapel Street filling water at the Spout around 1955. This photograph links up with one by Currey a century earlier. John was bringing water to Dennehy's on the Convent Road where he worked on the farm. Tensions often arose at the Spout over access culminating in 'The Battle of the Spout' around the mid-twentieth century.

Farming in 'Ashbourne' Townspark around 1930, reaping and binding. From left to right: Tess O'Farrell, Dick Ahearne, Paddy 'Lou' O'Farrell, Padjo Collins, Shaun O'Farrell and Paky Flynn.

Above left: A lovely portrait from 1900 of William Lineen and his wife Bridget (née Moore) from Ballyin. Bridget's family had been evicted by landlord Kiely-Ussher, however here we're looking at a proud resurgent lady in her lovely Spanish cloak with large satin-lined hood likely made by herself as a 'Lismore cloak'. Bill had a small farm in Ballyin and became a kind of Lineen paterfamilias; he had twelve children.

Above right: Joe O'Donnell at his hardware shop in Ferry Lane in the early 1940s. It is now Mrs Anne Whelan's. Joe moved to Geary's across the road in the 1950s, where he ran a very successful pub and hardware store. Mikey O'Donnell succeeded and retired in 2004 from business. It is now a video rental shop with the charming retro name of Flix.

A meitheal at the hay in Shrough in the mid 1940s. The meitheal (mihul) was or is simply a band of neighbouring farmers or voluntary workers coming together to help each other to thresh corn, cut turf, make hay and so on; food and hospitality was the reward for one's labour. As the saying went: 'hay-making days and the day of the turf – these are days to eat enough'. This meitheal was at Power's, Mrs Power to immeditae left.

Above left: The Foleys of Mayfield 1959. From left to right, back row: Mrs Hannah Foley and Katherine O'Brien. Front row: Mick, Jim and Joe Foley. Mick said the dog was deaf so they didn't name it.

Above right: The Hickey family in 1911 when they lived at No. 3 New Street. It includes Thomas and Hannah Hickey, children Mary (Mamie) and Tom – the latter to become a famous journalist and editor in the UK. Thomas Snr. worked as a carpenter at Lismore Estates.

J.P. Daly's shop front on Main Street. The proprietor J.P. sits with daughter Sheila on his knee while Mrs Daly stands longside. This photograph was taken in the 1920s, J.P. dying in 1939 when his son Redmond succeeded him. The shop is now the Gael Byrne Flower and Craft Gallery.

Sponsored walk in the late 1980s for Lismore CBS Post-Primary School. If education is a life-long experience, this school was only a short-time experiment. Mick O'Brien plays the 'box' as Br. Blake, Pad Vaughan, John Cunningham, J. Lineen and others walk the walk. Anne Vaughan, Peg Campion-Donovan and Mrs P. Vaughan at the Monument lend moral support.

Portrait of a Lady between two ricks and a Laird's place. Peggy O'Brien home on her parents' farm – Jerry O'Brien and Mrs O'Brien – at Monamon around 1950.

Children in Fernville 1944. From left to right, back row: Joe Martin, Des Frawley, Seamus Byrne, Frank Frawley, Rosie Murphy, Siobhan O'Donoghue and Mary O'Farrell. Front row: Lily Mason, Frank Mason, Finola Byrne, Margaret Frawley, Teresa Martin, Michael O'Farrell, Joan Boyle and Nena Boyle. Seamus Byrne and Michael O'Farrell had received their First Communion on that day.

Goulding's shop-front, the shop – a hardware and public house in the late 1920s. William Condon, the shop assistant, is at the door. This was the home of Seán Goulding, Chairman of the Irish Senate. De Valera was known to visit the house. Note the name 'Ua Guilidhe' which was likely a coinage of Seán's own, also the gaslight at the corner.

The Gay Twenties: a group on a day's social outing from Lismore. From left to right, back row (five men standing): –?–, Gordon Whelan, John Gillen, J. Stapleton and P. Murphy. Middle row (five men sitting): Tom Hickey, P. 'Malach' Regan, (the next three are thought to be members of the Heaphy family of Botany). Front row: P. Tierney (extreme left), –?–, G. Colbert, J. Meade, –?–. There is little enough information on this group. They are a filial rather than a particular works outing group. Some are Castle workers, others of diverse employment.

Two very typical Lismoreians of a bygone era namely Pad 'Fork' Doherty (left) of Church Lane and Tom 'Jap' O'Connor (Connors) of Round Hill. Tom was one of the 'Wavers' a family of weavers who came originally from Knockanore; others of the Waver or the 'wavering brotherhood' as described in Lismore's Millennium Journal being Jack, Pad, Tony, Mick and the father Phil.

Fred and Adele Astaire on the Main Drag in the 1950s. Autographed photograph of truly great ones who were regularly in Lismore, Adele having a child buried there. Look at them: they might start dancing and often did on roads around Lismore.

A swinging tea party in Cooldelane in 1957 at Begley's for visit home of USA based nun. From left to right, back row: Maisie Veale, Bridge Cullinane, Irene Begley, Margaret Walsh, Sr Teresa O'Farrell and Joe O'Farrell. Front row: Paddy O'Farrell, Tony Begley, Michael Begley, John Begley, Aileen Begley, Mary Begley, Jim Begley, Dick Mulcahy, and the small girl to front is Bridget Begley.

three

Transport

General View at Lismore Station in 1930. Lismore railway station was designed by Sancton Wood, who also designed Heuston station in Dublin. The Fermoy and Lismore Railway was an independent company financed by the Duke ('The Duke's Line') and opened in 1872. The Waterford Dungarvan & Lismore Railway (WD & LR) was opened in 1878 allowing passengers to get from Waterford to Lismore in 135 minutes. Apart from passengers and parcels, pigs bought by Fred Dennehy from Denny's, horse boxes for the races, coal for Noonan's, and cattle for fairs made up the traffic and in its heyday the Station employed sixteen.

Lismore Railway Station 1928. In this photograph Robert Chestnutt poses with his children, staff, and a porter from Blackwater Vale Hotel (now Roche's). Chestnutt was in Lismore for less than a decade and left in 1932. The gas fittings were still in situ but electricity was long in operation. Along the platform an old style bread van can be seen.

Right: Signal Box Lismore Railway Station in the 1920s. The man in front is Ca or 'Cuddy' Power ('Cuddy' was once popular in Lismore as a pet name, the origin embedded in Mochuda). The man at the back is not known.

Below: The consensus view (which can be wrong) is that this is Mayfield Railway level crossing awaiting the *Rosslare* in the late 1950s. Mayfield was operated by Dinny and Katie Power. Mrs Power was the real operator as she was an early 'worker from home': Dinny worked on hr railway and with the county council.

A view of the railway bridge which carried the trains over the old hospital road. It is interesting to compare the surrounds with other snaps of this once defining feature. Many remember jumping off it into passing carts of hay or wool.

The last train at Lismore Railway Station 1967. The line closed on 29 March 1967, after almost a century in operation. To the right stand Billy and Dick Power. Surely a heart-breaking day for many, including the Powers who were synonymous with the great railway tradition, for example, Dick Power worked for over thirty years at the station and was the last honorary stationmaster (Ned O'Connor was the last stationmaster to live in the House). Dick's grandfather was a ganger at the time of the opening of the line. The station later became a sausage casing factory and is now the excellent Centre for Traditional Skills run by the O'Neills.

Above: Waiting for the Express: Lismore's defunct station, 1969. This photograph was taken by Felix O'Neill of his wife Anne (O'Brien) on the line and a jennet on the platform. Even the jennet looks dejected at the prospect of never another train, perhaps hoping for some ghost train to end it all.

Right: Mrs Nugent and son of Ballyin off to town on the express transport of its day namely, 'God's parody on all four-footed things'. What style, what a gig, who wouldn't like to be aboard for this shopping expedition in the 1930s.

Above: The woman holding the donkey is Mrs Maggie Kiernan, and to her left is Mrs Nell Foley and son Bing. They are exiting the Castle sawmills around 1947 with bags of sawdust used for boiling offal to rear a few pigs for pin and other monies. The offal drums were five-gallon oil drums supplied gratuitously by Jim Feeney's garage in West Street.

Right: Working at Crownex with Horse and Dray. Crownex, a Dutch firm, set up a business making sausage casings for export after the Station's closure. Here we see Dick Power carting barrels.

Above: Jerry O'Sullivan with human cargo around 1952. Jerry worked for the County Council for many years. Jerry was no mere character, rather a personality with great humour and yarn telling capacity.

Right: The Fitzgerald family from Castle View North Mall setting out on a trip to the mountains in 1912. The McGraths subsequently lived in Castle View and now the Daly family. The photograph includes Larry and Mrs Fitzgerald and son Gerald. One can't help reflecting that the animal must have been something of a mountain of an animal itself if it carried so many!

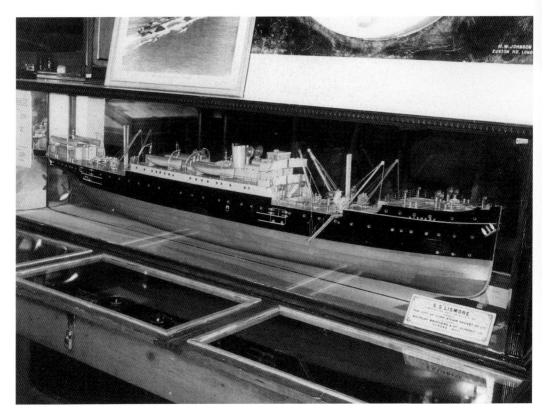

The S.S. *Lismore,* lost between Cork and Liverpool in 1906. The ship carried cattle and general cargo: it developed a list and sank with the loss of 18 of the 19 crew. John Carley, a young Wexford sailor, survived by making a make-shift raft and using his coat as a sail, he eventually made it to the Wexford coast. Carley was born with a caul, which meant according to folk belief he would never drown. The British Navy designed a raft called the Carley Raft in his honour: it was later superseded by the inflatable raft. This replica of the *Lismore* is in Dún Laoghaire Maritime Museum.

Opposite above: Four intrepid Lismoreians on Lady Louise's accommodation bridge over the Owennashad in the 1940s. From left to right: Jim Campion , Eddie Lynch (Chapel Street), Mick Ryan (Botany), Jim Stapleton. We say intrepid because from this time on the grand lady began to withdraw her accommodation as old age encroached.

Opposite below: Pioneers on a Jaunting Car Ride in Killarney in 1948. From left aboard jaunting car: Corney Willoughby, Moss Pollard, Jarvey, Jim Stapleton and two unknown boys. The PTA (Pioneer Total Abstinence Association) was begun by Fr Cullen towards the end of the nineteenth century. Fr Denis McGrath in Lismore was a powerful recruiting officer through the schools.

Left: Dervla Murphy of Lismore, travel writer, sets off again on her bike in Tibet 1966. Her transport is usually the most basic: shanks mare, bike, mule or donkey. A real traveller is Dervla; the rest of us are but tourists – failed travellers. Dervla's writing is exceptionally lucid and insightful. To read her is to travel with her: it's as real as virtual reality gets.

John Scott Allen Fernville at the wheel, in the late 1920s. John succeeded his father as organist at St Carthage's Church of Ireland Cathedral. His era was the era of the piano. John made a living buying, selling and tuning pianos. He was also an expert salmon and trout angler. John died in 1957, his wife died in 2004.

four

War and
Peace

The LDF (Local Defence Forces) pictured here during the Second World War. The LDF was formed to help the Gardaí. Each Garda district trained six volunteer groups and an extra armed group to guard the Gardaí and vital installations. Most opted for the armed group and were deemed military. Lightly armed at first, they later acquired Enfield and Springfield rifles. By 1943 the LDF numbered 103,000, representing the various units such as artillery, cavalry, signals and so on. The LDF became the FCA (Fórsa Cosanta Áitiúil) in 1947.

The LDF marching on Main Street during The Emergency in 1942. A kind of Irish 'Dad's Army' of volunteers and raw recruits who were, of course, highly motivated and committed to serve the Free State. The boy, second right in front, is likely Mick Neville.

Right: Edward Landers was born in Ballinvella, Lismore in 1881. He became a shoemaker and had his own shop in Church Lane. One of the first committed activists of Lismore Company Irish Volunteers, he was arrested in 1920 and interned in Ballykinlar Camp though married with four children. As a prisoners' leader he was badly wounded on 19 June 1922. Sadly his wife was refused leave to travel north to see him. He died on 23 June 1922. A huge crowd met his remains in Lismore on Sunday 26 June 1922. He was interred in the old cemetery in Lismore, where a limestone monument marks his grave.

Below left: Gravestone of Thomas Greehy (Tomás Ó Gríofa), Patriot. Thomas Greehy was born in Church Lane. An excellent student, he joined the Lismore Company of the Volunteers and was extremely active. Fighting on the republican side in the Civil War, he was killed at Kilwatermoy in a cruel booby-trap mine in March of 1923. A monument marks where he was killed. This gravestone is in St Carthage's Cemetery.

Above right: Gravestone of James Lawlor, killed 1920. A train driver from Inchicore he was shot at Goulding's Corner in 1920 by a sentry. An accidental victim of war, he is buried longside Thomas Greehy in St Carthage's Cemetery.

The Boy Scout movement in Lismore was started by Fr Thomas A. Murphy in 1934, the Girl Guides a little later. Henry Collins was the first scout master with his able assistant Jack O'Donnell. They flourished under Pad Walsh and Kieran Fenton as leaders but collapsed around 1952 when Kieran Fenton bowed out. A revival in the 1970s was attempted but didn't last. This photograph shows members of the Ninth Battalion, Catholic Boy Scouts in Youghal at a summer camp. From left to right, back row: John Crotty, Andy Coleman, Jackie Walsh and John Scanlan. Middle row: Pad Walsh S.M., Peter O'Brien, Seán Dennis, Mick Scanlan, Terry Forde, Richard Broderick, Mick Feeney and Seán O'Connell. Front row: Michael Coleman, John Hickey, Joe Martin, Raymond Burke, Patsy Bray, Bernard Walsh, Willie Walsh and Billy O'Brien.

Above left: Patrick Mangan (Pádraig Ó Mangáin) was born in Carrignagour in 1900. He became a Volunteer with Lismore Company whose HQ was at Jerry O'Brien's, Monamon. On the republican side after the Treaty, he was shot dead in Cork Jail in 1922 while negotiating to end a jail protest. He is buried in the catholic section of the Church of Ireland graveyard.

Above right: P.J. Hickey, Gunner Royal Field Artillery, killed March 1919. Hickey was from Glencairn and was 24 when he died. This gravestone is in the old cemetery on Chapel steet.

Right: John Duggan of Chapel Street fought with the US army in the Second World War. He was awarded the Silver Star twice. Seen here is Seamus Furey, Vietnam War Veteran. Seamus a nephew of John Duggan. Not a man to dodge the draft he too served with distinction and honour despite, the futility of the Vietnam conflict. He now lives in semi-retirement in Youghal.

Below: The Volunteer Certificate of Tim Duggan, 1917. Tim was an organizer of the Volunteers and Commanding Officer of the Second Battalion West Waterford Brigade. Joe Duggan, brother of Tim, is still alive and well and is considered by many hurling critics to be Waterford's best ever hurler. Tim Duggan died in 1952.

Left: Two musical scouts from the earliest era of scouting in Lismore. Mick Keating (left) on the 'box' and Dick Power on the fiddle. The backdrop is Tom Crean's old home in Botany where the hooley was likely in progress.

Below: Gravestone of Matthew Kavanagh, MBE. A Chapel Street man. He was awarded the MBE (Member of the Order of the British Empire) by Queen Elizabeth II. A fine outstanding man who honoured Lismore abroad.

Éamon de Valera speaking in Lismore in the General Election of 1947-1948. After the meeting Ned Coleman (butcher at McGrath's) was heard to say, 'The man who shouted *Up Dev* the loudest had a big patch in his pants!'

The unveiling of a monument to those who fought in the War of Independence, on the Melleray Road in 1966. From left to right: Guard Houlihan from Lismore, Vincent O'Donoghue (wearing old IRA medal) giving the address, and Pádraig Ó Fionnghúsa from Cappoquin.

Above left: The Three O'Farrells and Horst. From left to right, back row: Mary O'Farrell, Horst Selzener, and Kathleen O'Farrell. Front: Eithne O'Farrell. The O'Farrells lived in Ardagh in Fernville. Horst was a refugee child from Germany after the Second World War. He returned home after about two years and still lives in Germany.

Above right: Guard Paddy Martin and Josie Condon (The Red House) in Chapel Street, in front of Quinlan's shop around 1930. We can easily see that the snap captures old time policing - community policing.

Eoin O'Duffy speaking at a United Ireland Party meeting in Lismore, in January 1934. The UIP was the original name of Fine Gael and an amalgam of Cumann na nGael, the Centre Party and the National Guard (Blueshirts). In the background Gold Cup tea is advertised but there is no evidence of the later famous Raleigh sign and slogan as Gaeilge: 'An rothar déanta de chruaidhe ar fad!'

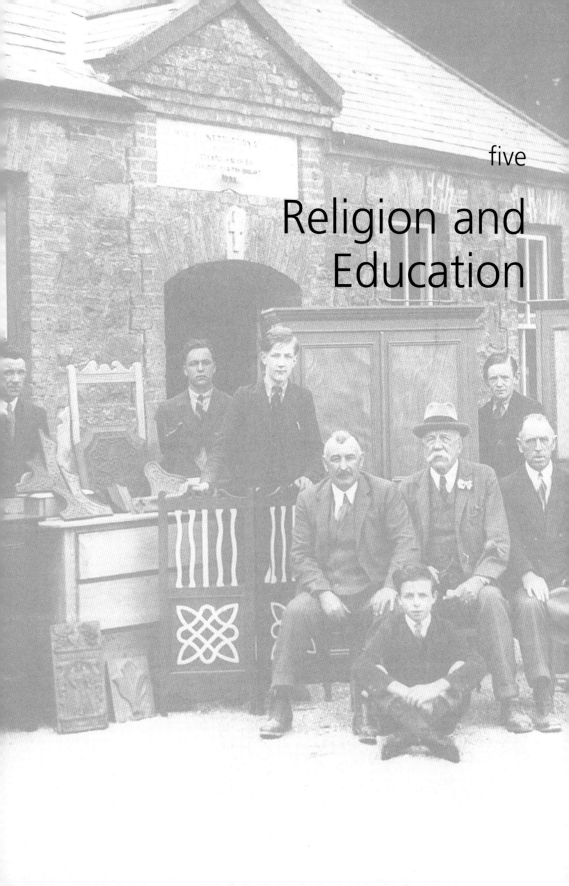

five

Religion and
Education

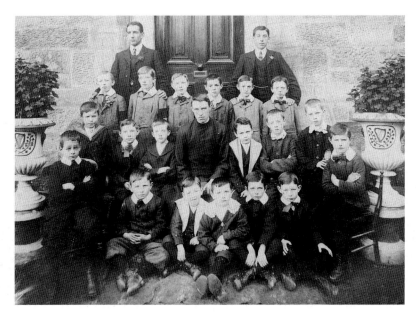

Earliest CBS Photo. Very little is known of the provenance of this photo, but it is felt to be the earliest of the photos taken with a Christian Brothers' theme. Taken in front of the Monastery well over one hundred years ago, the students are remarkable for their propriety of dress, nor do the teachers exhibit any casualness. Solemnity was the watchword of education at that time.

Juniors taken at Lismore Convent around 1912. From left to right, back row: John O'Donnell (Fernville), Dan Byrne (Round Hill), Jack Sullivan (Fernville), and Tom O'Connor. (Note that all four of the line became priests bar Jack Sullivan.) Middle row: Margaret M. Walshe (Fishery, later Feeney's garage), Moll Heaphy, Maggie Doyle (Botany), –?–, Francie Connors (Fernville). Front row: Bridie Ormonde, Lizzie Lynch (Church Lane), Annie O'Connell (Fernville) Lily Forde, Lily May Morrissey, Katy O'Brien (Nun), Aggie Connors (Fernville) and Teasie O'Brien (East Main Street).

A Holy Family: The Mangans of Carrignagour. From left to right, back row: Dr Peter Mangan (Loyola University), Fr (Monsignor) Bernard Mangan, Fr Joe Mangan and Fr Dominic Mangan. Front row: Sr Bernadette Mangan and Sr Mercedes Mangan.

A class of Presentation Convent girls from around 1915. From left to right, back row: Mary O'Donnell, Annie Gillen, Lena Prendergast, Nina McCarthy (Geary), Katie Ahearne, Hannah Broderick (Sr Carthage), Teresa Meade, Mary Condon. Front row : Marcella Beirne, Zillah Wright, Elsie Morrissey, Gussie O'Brien (Nun, USA), Mary Ellen O'Connell, Chris O'Donnell, Teresa O'Gorman, Maggie O'Gorman (Sr Benignus), Lily Baker.

Left: Sr Carthage Broderick (left) entered the Presentation nuns in 1918 and died in 1940. Mother Benignus O'Gorman entered the same time and died in 1975. Both were born within a stone's throw of each other in Ballyin–Monatarive and now lie buried a few yards from each other in the nuns' graveyard, kindly preserved by Hanley's, next to the now-defunct Convent. Mother Benignus had the distinction of being the only nun to be three times Reverend Mother in Lismore.

Below: A combined muster of Primary and Secondary Schools at CBS in the late 1920s. At almost extreme left we see Br Carey and behind him W. Devine who became an Oblate Father. On the third row, fifth from left is N. O'Connell, and second row sixth from left is Johnny Vaughan. On the extreme right is E. Scully, teacher and on the third step of the stairs is Vincent O'Donoghue, teacher.

Display of Woodwork (Evening Class) at CBS Manual School in the 1920s.
From left to right: Two proud instructors, Frank O'Donnell, Michael
McGrath, Eddie Nugent. Seated: Pakes O'Brien (Botany).

This school photo is from the late 1920s and was touched up from a damaged
original. The pupils are first years at the Presentation Convent under the Tutelage
of Miss Eva Wright, on the right. From left to right, back row: Mick Bransfield,
Edward Foley, Mick Lineen, Jim Power and Tommy Scanlan. Next row: Hannah
power, Nell Hennessy, bridie creedon, Maisie Quirke, -?-, ? Scanlan, Norah Clancy,
and ? Crowley. Next Row: Kathy O'Donnell, AgnesSheehan, mona O'Connell,
B. Lineen, -?-, Mary Willoughby, Dorothea Daly and Mary Flynn. Front Row: P.
Wlash, Joe Duggan, Frank Tierney, -?-, Mik Dobson, T. Ryan and Ca O'Donnell.

St Carthage's Catholic Parish Church is considered to be the most handsome in the diocese. Made from local sandstone and limestone dressings in the Romanesque style, it looks graceful and welcoming. It was consecrated in 1884. The architect was Walter Doolin and the builders Messrs. Redmond of Wexford. The Campanile is 120ft high in the North Italian style and within, monolithic columns of red Aberdeen granite, along with Portland stone capitals, carry the arches. It cost £12,000 to build, mostly donated by the parishioners. This 1930s view shows the fine wrought iron gates removed in the 1933 renovations and Canon Fogarty's headstone also removed later.

First Communion at Lismore Convent, 1930. This day was often the most memorable of people's childhood. Apart from the religious aspect, it is too, a developmental milestone. In those days, the two-egg breakfast at the Convent and the prospect of getting one's 'Communion money' were also important. From left to right, back row: P. Vaughan, P. O'Farrell, P. Feeney J. O'Donoghue, M. Dobson, F. Tierney, J. Coghlan, M. Walsh, T. Ryan. Front row: W. Ryan, T. Coleman, B. Kennefick, F. McCarthy, C. Willoughby, P. Harty, M. Hartnett, L. Power, M. Keyes, T. Russell.

A fine view of the Eucharistic Procession of June 1953. Note the prominence of the girl guides and their leadership roles.

A stylish wedding in St Ozburg's Church in Coventry of Billy Neville of Lismore and Gene Mulligan of Mullingar, April 1959. From left to right: Henry Neville, S. Mulligan, Jo Stapleton, Alice Neville, Kathleen Neville, Mrs Kit Neville, Michael Neville, Mrs Mulligan, Eily Neville, Tina Mulligan, M. Mulligan, Philip Neville.

A Class of Presentation Convent girls from around 1927. From left to right, back row: Kathleen Cullinane, Mary B. Lineen, Agnes Healy, Teresa O'Connell, Cissie O'Keeffe, Gertie O'Connell, Isa Rice, Eily McCarthy, Mary Teresa O'Keeffe, Eily Conlon, Mary Vaughan, Mary Canning and Mary O'Sullivan. Middle row: Nellie Greehy, Irene Cullinane, Margaret Walsh, Mary Aherne, Monica Meade, Elicia Murphy, L. McCarthy, Teresa Cashman, Mary Paul Murray, Mary Morrissey and Bridie McCarthy. Front row : Maggie Foley (Ballyduff), Hannah Lawton, Betty Vaughan, Peggy Foley, Kathleen Coffey, Agnes Walsh, Mary McCarthy, Monsy Sweeney, Nora Farrell and Nellie O'Donoghue.

A Class Photo from the Presentation Convent, 1930s. From left to right, back row: Mary A. Doherty, Mary Nugent, Mary O'Donnell, Biddy Devine, May Quinn, Sheila Courtney, Bridie Maloney, Sheila Daly, Kitty Callaghan and Anna Walsh. Middle row: Annie Lawton, Emmie Russell, Mary Daly, Mary O'Neill, Kitty O'Connell, Eva Wright (Teacher), M. Crotty, Eily Healy, Norrie Foley, Manny Keyes and Bridie Nugent. Front row: Kitty Conlon, Dolly Chestnutt, Mary Willoughby, Cecelia Foley, Maudie Power, Peace O'Brien, M. Kelleher and Nellie Campion.

Ordination of Fr Mikey Coleman, Cootehill, Co. Cavan 1958. From left to right: Andy Coleman, Fr Mikey Coleman, Dr O'Callaghan, ordaining Bishop, and Mrs Coleman.

Leaving Certificate Class, Lismore CBS, 1945-1946. From left to right, back row: M. McGrath (Camphire), Noel Collender, Bill Lineen, John Dower (Aglish), Noel Foley. Front row : D. O'Shea (Tallow), Joe Hanrahan, Jack Healy, B. O'Brien (Tallow). Missing from the photo is Andy Coleman.

An Experimental Science class in the form of nature-study being conducted at Lismore CBS under the tutelage of Vincent O'Donoghue. The tall student to his left is Moss Fives.

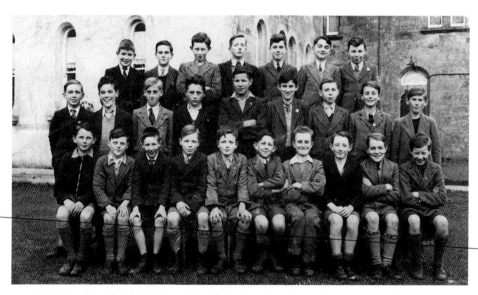

Class photograph of first year and part of second years at Lismore CBS Secondary School taken in October 1946. Note that it was still the era of short pants worn for longer years! From left to right, back row: John Murphy, Seán O'Connell, John Joe O'Donnell, Noel Doocey, Billy O'Brien, Michael Twomey and Michael Madden. Middle row: Michael Feeney, Jim Lineen, Bob McCarthy, Tom Ryan, Paddy Walsh, Paddy Ballantyne, Michael O'Farrell (Ashbourne), John Arrigan and Joe Daly. Front row: Brian McSweeney, Walter Crean, Michael Coleman, Pat O'Donoghue, Maurice Hickey, Paddy Browne, Billy Stack, Michael Troy, Michael (Coz) Madden and Bernard Lonergan.

Ballinavella National School in the mid-1930s. This photo includes Paddy Pender and Mrs Eily Hennessy (Teacher, extreme right). The school was closed in the amalgamation era and is today a community centre.

A view of the Eucharistic Procession going up Gallows Hill around 1940. First line nearest camera, reading from right to left: J. Vaughan, M. Whelan, G. O'Brien, C. Murray, M. Mason, J. Cunningham, M. Gough . Second line: John Kenneally, B. Sheehan, –?–, T. Lyons, M. O'Brien, Billy Broderick, Tommy Healy, B. Power, D. Behegan. Third line: T. Scanlan, P. Power, D. Condon. Fourth line: M. Scanlan, T. Hartnett. Note also the number of men wearing confraternity medals.

Left: 'Going to Mass' in 1959. Jim Baldwin (left) and Johnny Foley. Jim died recently in his nineties: a man who evoked a poem for his sheer character. He raised being a hardware assistant to a fine art.

Below: Display of Woodwork, Evening Class at CBS Manual School in the 1930s. The youth standing fourth left is Patrick Geoghegan who won first prize in Ireland for his work. A brilliant student who became a Creamery Manager (the Glen Farm influence) but tragically died young. Third from right is Frank O'Donnell (a man intent on evening classes that yielded furniture). The behatted teacher is Tom Halpin while the man second left at back is Tommy McCarthy, also a teacher. Close scrutiny of the items shows how intricate and detailed the wood-carving is.

Above left: Monsignor Terence O'Brien was born in 1916 in Lismore and schooled there. Ordained priest in 1943 by Bishop Staunton for the Los Angles Archdiocese. He was finally Parish Priest of St Juliana's Fullerton. He retired to Ireland and died in 1999 and is buried in the churchyard of St Carthage's Cathedral.

Above right: First Sunday at Mass for Young Breda Hennessy, 7 June 1959. Mrs Joan Hennessy, Bishopstown inducts her four-year-old reluctant Catholic daughter at St Carthage's Cathedral. Behind, some devout sceptics foregather in front of Kelly's. Third left is certainly Jim Baldwin, New Street while fifth left is Johnny Foley. Breda is married to J.J. Duggan and lives in Tourin.

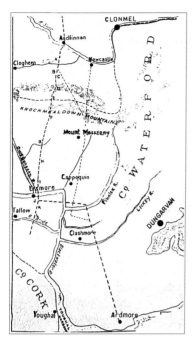

Previous page below: Open Air Mass in St Declan's cemetery on Walsh's farm in Dromroe to celebrate St Declan's feast day, which falls on 24 July. Dromroe is the birthplace of St Declan, a little over a mile east of Lismore. St Declan is the patron saint of the Diocese of Waterford and Lismore and founded a famous monastery in Ardmore.

Left: Map showing Bóthar na Naomh and Rian Bó Phádraig. Lismore, being so important, was linked to Cashel, the great ecclesiastical centre by another roadway called Rian Bó Phádraig (The Track of St Patrick's Cow). This Rian intersected with Bóthar na Naomh near or at Round Hill. The road derived its name from the folk story that a calf, owned by St Patrick, was stolen in south Tipperary and brought into Co Waterford. Its mother followed the rustler, gouging out a passageway with her horns – so impassioned was her maternal instinct – until she found the calf and exacted revenge. Of course there is little hard evidence that St Patrick was ever in Lismore but parts of Rian Bó Phádraig are still visible (e.g. off the main Lismore-Cappoquin Road), though most has been obliterated by tillage.

Confirmation class at the Presentation Convent, 29 May 1955. From left to right, back row: Nora Keane, Margaret Buckley, Dolly Whelan, Catherine Whelan, Claire Lineen, Chrissie Neville, Ann Hickey, Betty Carroll, Mary Moynihan, Mary O'Brien, Pauline Keane and Dolores Hickey. Middle row: Kay Milward, Mary Foley, Catherine O'Brien, Elaine Glasse, Mary McGrath, Kathleen O'Brien, Alice Neville, Helen Murphy, Josie Hale and Kathleen O'Gorman. Front row: Rena O'Connor, Cepta Power, Margaret Murphy, Martha Dunne, Joan O'Donovan, Anne Cahill, Helen Fleming, Eileen Ross and Mary Fleming.

Class of 1950/51 Lismore Presentation Convent. From left to right, back row: Rosie Murphy, Bridie Lineen, Kathleen Heskin, Bernie Sargent, Betty Nolan, Pat Fraher, May Browne. Front row: Maureen Russell, Marjorie Meaney, Peg Cashin, Siobhan O'Donoghue, Eily O'Sullivan and Eily Cotter.

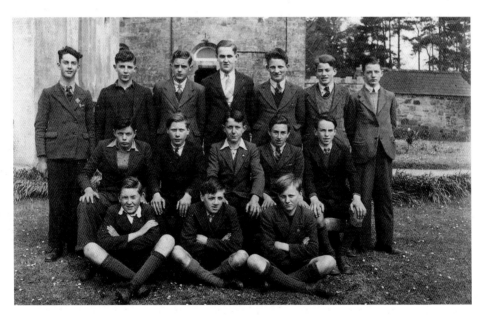

A school group at Lismore CBS in the mid 1940s. From left to right, back row: Finbarr Kearney, Billy Neville, John Geoghegan, Ben Carey, Jim Fives, Kevin Maloney and John Crotty. Middle row: Noel Collender, Paddy Barry, Michael Brown , Jim Lawless, William Maloney. Front row: Richard Mason, Tony Bransfield and John Noonan.

A Vintage Class photo from Lismore Convent around 1956. From left to right, back row: Marie Barry (Glencairn), Mary O'Keeffe, Ann O'Connor, Ann Moynihan, Margaret Feeney, Sheila Keating, Joan Dahill (Glencairn), Teresa O'Gorman, Elsie Baldwin, Front row: Phyllis O'Donovan, Margaret O'Donnell, Sister Frances, Toinette Howard and Gwen Dunne.

Class photo at Lismore Convent Secondary School 1963. From left to right, back row: Dolly Mills (Kilwatermoy), Susie McGrath (Camphire), Aileen O'Brien, Eileen Geoghegan (Ballyduff), Mary Tobin (Monalour) and Ena O'Sullivan. Middle row: Kathleen Hallahan, Olive Fleming, Patricia Kearney, Kathy Wilkinson, Mary Ross, Kitty O'Gorman (Ballyin), Beatrice McCarthy (Tallow). Front row: Mary Fenton (Tallow), Catherine and Norah Dunne (Ballinraha), June Murphy, June Landers (Camphire).

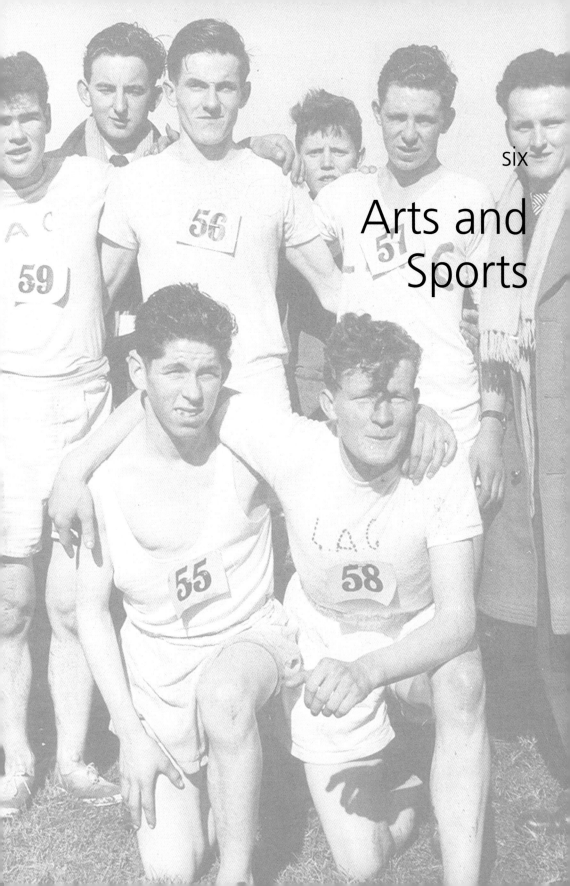

six

Arts and
Sports

Above: Lismore Coursing Club at the Monument in 1938. The group looks completely invulnerable, 'the law an-all' on board. From left to right throughout: Jack Devine, Jim 'Sergeant' Keating, Guard Purcell, K. Fenton, Sgt Ballantyne, John O'Sullivan, Paddens Ryan, Ned Fenton, Jack O'Sullivan, Tim Duggan, John O'Gorman, Liam Power, Bill Power, T. O'Brien (obscured), Jacko Keyes, Jimmy Foley, John Foley, Mick O'Gorman, Jimmy O'Neill, Jack O'Gorman, Bob Lineen.

Left: This is a fine study of Cyril Hynes MRCVS. Cyril qualified as a veterinary surgeon or vet in 1905 and started practice in Lismore as the town's first vet in 1906. He travelled extensively to clients initially in a gig. He also ran Lismore's first cinema in the South Mall. Cyril was a fine golfer and a clay pigeon shooting champion too.

Lismore Blackwater Ramblers 1898: the classic pose, the ultimate ensemble. Gaelic football teams were 17 a-side at this time. The Ramblers grew to be a peerless outfit and have become legendary. Their golden era lasted about two decades; then the 'brethren of the sliotar' (hurlers) began to rule. From left to right, back row: P. Heelan, N. Regan, -?-, T. O'Donoghue, N. Murphy, -?-, V. O'Brien. (The missing names could be any of: M. Lyons, D. Donovan, ? Cotter or M. Power). Middle row: P. Whelan, J. Bennett, W. Hogan, J.C. Heelan, 'Brickie' Flynn, P. Murphy and P. Power. Front: -?-, J. Vaughan, J. Baldwin and P. Foley

Those launching tennis in the Community Centre site in 1988 called their club the newest in town, in fact it was one of the older ones as this photo from the 1930s shows. The group includes; Noreen (Norrie) O'Riordan, the Foleys, Isa Rice-McGrath and Peadar and Joan Hickey.

Above: Presentation to retiring postman Mick O'Brien at Meagher's of Ballysaggart May 1971. A remarkable ordinary man the late Mick: freedom fighter, fine musician and hurler, but above all great family man and Lismoreian. Back row from left to right (10): Mick O'Brien, John Fennessy, Mick Coleman, Chris O'Brien, Pat Foley, -?-, Eugene O'Brien, -?-, Billy Foley and Mike O'Neill (hatted with glasses). Next row (9): Breda Foley, Pad Fennessy, Janie O'Brien, Tom Hale, Noreen Foley, Mary Dunne, Kath Neville, Paddy Dunne and Jim Clancy. Middle group (16): Jim Roche, Dick Lyons, Marty McNamara, Patsy Carey, Mick Greehy, Mamie Carey, Pad Nugent, Mary Fennessy (behind J. Murphy), Maur O'Brien (front of Breda Foley), -?-. Mrs Hallahan (front of Pad Fennessy), Maggie O'Sullivan, Kit Neville, Kath O'Brien, Philip Neville and Geraldine Dunne. Next row (8): John Daly, Mrs K. Murphy, Mrs K. McNamara, Mrs. E. Murphy, John Murphy, Nell Foley, Dodo Lyons and M. Dunne. Front row: Mrs E. Meagher and son Benny. Brendan Meagher makes the presentation.

Above: This fancy dress photo from 1954 of, from left: David, Michael and Geraldine McGrath recalls An Tóstal or the 'Ireland at Home to the World' Festival of the time. An Tóstal was essentially a wake-up call to the potential of Ireland as a tourist venue.

Right: The cast of *Columbus in a Merry Key*, a CBS drama production of 1948. From left to right, back row: Walter Crean (Head Philosopher), Mickey O'Farrell ('Banana Bill') and Mick Feeney (Mademoiselle Sago Palm). Front row: Jim Lineen (The Caribee King), Jim Ballantyne (Queen Isabella of Spain), Brian McSweeney (King Ferdinand of Spain). A real hoot of a show by all accounts and beautifully recalled by Jim Ballantyne in his book, *Lismore: Autobiography of an Irish Town 1937-1954*.

Lismore Fife and Drum Band in the early 1930s. These kinds of bands proliferated prior to the onset of mass entertainment. From left to right, back row,: Seamus Ryan, -?-, Fr M. Walsh, E. Collins, J. Power, J. O'Sullivan, B. Keyes, P. Pollard and J. Creagh. Middle row: B. O'Brien, P. Keyes, P. Stapleton, J. Grady, Jim Ahearne, Bob Lynch, J. Singleton, J. Foley, E. Pollard, M. Crowley, Bob Creagh, and T. Landers. Front row: T. Duggan, Jack Landers, Pat O'Brien, Chris O'Brien and Jim Landers.

A Lismore cricket team of 1937. From left to right, back row: Willie Power, Jack Feeney, Dinny Byrne (Church Lane), J 'Jocklin' O'Donnell and Chris Whelan. Front row: Paddy 'Snobby' Barry, Jim Casey, Tom Duggan and Joe 'Kiely' Collins.

Above: From part of the set for the BBC film *One of Ourselves* made in 1983 and directed by ex-Lismoreian Pat O'Connor. Extras from left to right: 'Paddy 'the Gentleman' Connors (O'Connor), Paddy 'the Greater Gentleman' Connors, two Feeney sisters, Dick Canning, Danny Murray, Michael 'Mixer' Ahearne. The Wills's sign is a relic of Campion's old shop in Botany, the shop or pub being Biddy Greehy's. For the record, the child in the pram was Vicky Kiernan.

Right: Neighbours is a work by Julia M. Crottie, novelist and journalist, 1853-1934. Educated at the Presentation Convent, she spent most of her life on the Isle of Man, but is buried in the family plot in the old graveyard on Chapel Street. *Neighbours* is a book of short stories. The real character in the book is Innisdoyle, a small dull town which is undeniably Lismore in fictional guise.

NEIGHBOURS

By

JULIA M. CROTTIE

LONDON
T. FISHER UNWIN
PATERNOSTER SQUARE
1900

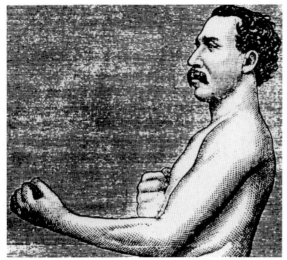

Ned O'Baldwin was born and raised on Main Street, Lismore (now Bets Daly's grocery) in 1840. He boxed first in England and was even matched with the great Jem Mace, but the bout was cancelled. Going to America, John Morrissey tested him in a twenty-minute sparring match with gloves. Ned floored Morrissey twice, a portent of his pugilistic talent. O'Baldwin was known as 'The Irish Giant', standing at near 6 ft 6 inches and fought at fifteen stone. He was recognised too, as a giant of the 'brethren of the thudding fists' and was virtual world champion, having beaten Joe Wormwald in 1868.

Denis Heskin, taken at his original home in Aglish Glencairn on board True Minstrel, winner of the Cobs' National at Punchestown. Denis was the son of Alex Heskin, a prominent Irish Party member. He was first elected to the Dáil as TD (Teachta Dála, MP) for Waterford in 1943. A popular sportsman and breeder and owner of fine chasers. He bred and trained forty seven Point-to-Point winners in eleven years.

Right: *Curlews* is a book of poems by
Temple Lane (pseudonym of Mary Isabel
Leslie), 1899-1982, novelist and poet.
Lane wrote some fine novels, one of them
Friday's Well (1943), being a best seller
and another, *The Little Wood*, winning the
Tailteann Literary Prize in 1932. A woman
of fine academic distinction holding a
doctorate from TCD, she died in 1982 and
is buried in Lismore.

Below: Youngsters messing at Lismore
Point-to-Point Races in the 1920s. Some
of the 'messers' were the children of Cyril
Hynes, Lismore's first Veterinary Surgeon.

CURLEWS

By

TEMPLE LANE

THE TALBOT PRESS LIMITED
EIGHTY-NINE TALBOT STREET, DUBLIN

Above: Celebrating the Centenary of the GAA in 1984. Here we see, from left, accordionists Billy Hogan, Mick Landers and Mick O'Brien leading the Centenary Parade. Following on are drummer boys Dick and Mick 'Mixer' Ahearne. Then, bearing crest, is Pat Lineen, and John Flynn just parading, while Tony Ahearne and Christy O'Brien bear the Lios Mór banner.

Left: Joe Whelan, outstanding athlete of his time, was also a talented gymnast. He is unique in that he was effectively an Olympian, having being selected for the Olympics in the 1920s, though he didn't compete. He dominated army distance running over nearly two decades. His sons Tom and Harry and especially Paddy were all great runners. He gave back in full measure to athletics and was an outstanding fisherman too.

Lismore Dramatic Society members relaxing during rehearsals at Ansons's in 1901. Lismore Dramatic Society (LDS) was founded in 1898. Early records are scarce however from 1940 on a grand variety concert was presented at St Patrick's Day and a play on 8th December. The theatre was, and still is, in the town hall. However the Happydrome was used on occasion. It was decided to go 'Panto' in 1975 and *Cinderella* was presented to great acclaim in 1977. An outstanding society, under the current leadership of Billy Devine.

The Brideside Serenaders. An early boy-band, but what boys, what music, what memories! From left to right, back row: Pete Gillen, Billy Hogan, Paddy Geary and Frank Pender. Front row: Ned O'Brien, Frankie Walsh (Manager), Jim Pender

Above: Lismore Junior County Hurling Champions 1924. This team represents an early flowering of hurling in Lismore. Recall that Mick O'Brien had seen his first hurley in jail during the Civil War. Though Lismore won the hurling county title during title in 1925-1926. From left to right, back row: J. O'Gorman, M. O'Brien, J. O'Brien, J. Doherty, J. Brien and M. Ormond. Middle row: J. Murphy, B. Neville, B. Hogan, J. Heaphy, J. Duggan and J O'Brien. Front row; A. Foley, H.(J.) Foley, D. Ormonde and J. Hogan. Soemmmentors at the back are: W. Hogan first left, Gordon Whelan (left of G'O'Gorman), Paddens Ryan (left of M. O'Brien), John 'Skinner' Power (left of J. O'Brien), P. Flynn (left of J. Doherty), B. Fitzgerald (right of J. Doherty) and J. Dunne (Hurling Field Lodge: Last man to right).

This photo records the culmination of years of dedicated athletics effort in Lismore: mad rushing round the Canon's field, birds' wings fluttering inside chest as feet pounded along Ard na Gaoithe, emitting guts in the corners of many indifferent fields. Ace mentor Joe Whelan egging on and Dinny Power with stop watch he assured you never stopped for slow coaches. And then the reward at Cleaboy 1956/57 as Lismore sweep the boards in the youths and have a vintage year all-round. After years of effort the club declined and was revived in 1983 with John Cahill an inspiration and fine athletes like Rena Carey, Michael Mulimphy, Patricia Cahill, Joan Coleman and Valerie Barry. Our photo shows, from left to right, back row: Joe Whelan, Val Foley, Jimmy O'Gorman, Pat Foley, John Whelan, Michael Twomey (No. 57, Ballyduff), Johnny Feeney, Tommy 'Bomber' Whelan. Front: Paddy Whelan, Timmy Murphy.

Opposite below: Ballysaggart first GAA (Gaelic Athletic Association) social in Lawlor's Hotel Dungarvan 1966. From left to right, back row: Dave Fennessy, Jimmy Greehy, Joe Roche, Mick Clancy, Tom Walsh, Joe Fahy (partly hidden), John Roche, Tommy Veale, Liam O'Gorman and Eamon Brackett. Front row: Mary Fennessy, Nora Walshe, Breda Stack, Kathleen Roche and Kitty Veale. Though the first social as such the Club was near eighty years old and won the first ever Waterford County Football Championship.

The Irish Hockey Union developed out of the Irish Hurling Union. Ireland participated in the first international hockey match ever against Wales and won Triple Crowns prior to and after the Second World War. This snap includes Cronie O'Gorman. Jack Heelan, Vincent Noonan, Jim Browne and bill Bolster (after whom the Bolster Cup was named), and David 'Boysie' Noonan.

Lismore accordion band on the occasion of the opening of the Gaelic pitch after improvement works in 1944. From left to right, back row,: J. Griffin, T. O'Donoghue, P. Gillen Jnr, P. Murray, P. Flynn, N. Murphy, Bill Landers. Middle row: D. Colbert, J. O'Brien (Melleray), F. Tierney, P. O'Brien, D. Power, J. Bennett, P. Stapleton, P. Bennett, M. Doherty, J. Behegan, M. Keating, Jim 'Slog' Ahearne , Joe Kelly and P. Walsh. Front row: P. Tierney, J. Flynn, T. Keating, T. Mangan, M. Landers, Matty Power, P. Gillen Snr and P. Scanlan. Sitting in front: J. Hickey, Billy Neville, W. Walsh, B. Hogan (printer), M. Scanlan and M. Feeney.

The first winners of the Senior County Championship, 1925. From left to right, back row: B. Hickey, Guard Walsh, Guard O'Rourke, J. Foley, Guard Murphy, Guard Moloney and P. Hickey. Middle row: B. Neville, B. Fitzgerald, P. Pyan, J. Ormonde. Front row: J. Ormonde, B .Hogan, J. Murphy, M. O'Brien.

Lismore CBS Hackett Cup winners of 1940. The Hackett Cup was competed for in the Diocese of Waterford and Lismore only, the Cup honoured the memory of Bishop Bernard Hackett. Lismore beat Mount Sion by two points in the final in Carrick-on-Suir in a stirring contest, one of the stars on the day being Pad Vaughan. From left to right, back row, (seven mentors and five players): J. Vaughan, Mannix Fenton (with flag), P. McCarthy, C. Willoughby, J. O'Gorman, B. Broderick, Br Duggan, J. Bransfield, J. Kavanagh (teacher), Jim Campion, John Pollard, B. Drohan (edging into J. Pollard). Middle row: T. Hancock (Tallow), Moss Fives, Pad Vaughan, Joe Duggan, F. McCarthy, Ed 'Goncey' Foley, D. 'Bud' Forde. Front row: M. Broderick, J. O'Donoghue, three youngsters in middle, Seán O'Connell, Ger & Pat O'Donoghue, T. McGrath, J. Lineën. The child to left is Seamus Byrne, son of Guard Byrne.

Left: Henry Wilson Grattan Flood 1857-1928, musicologist. Flood's great book is, A History of Irish Music (1905). He wrote books on the harp and bagpipes and edited Moore's Melodies. He coined the term uilleann pipes and showed how The Star Spangled banner is an O'Carolan air and how Celtic musicians developed the pentatonic scale. Pope Pius XI made him a Chevalier or Knight. Flood is Lismore's greatest man of the arts. He is buried in Enniscorthy.

Left: In this rare photo of the Guests we see Charlie the famous cyclist on the right, also his brother Claud and their mother. Charlie is held to be the first individual to bring a national title to Lismore. His cycling achievements are legendary and his sideboard was said to resemble a jeweller's shop, spilling into a haberdashery. This photograph was taken, around 1938.

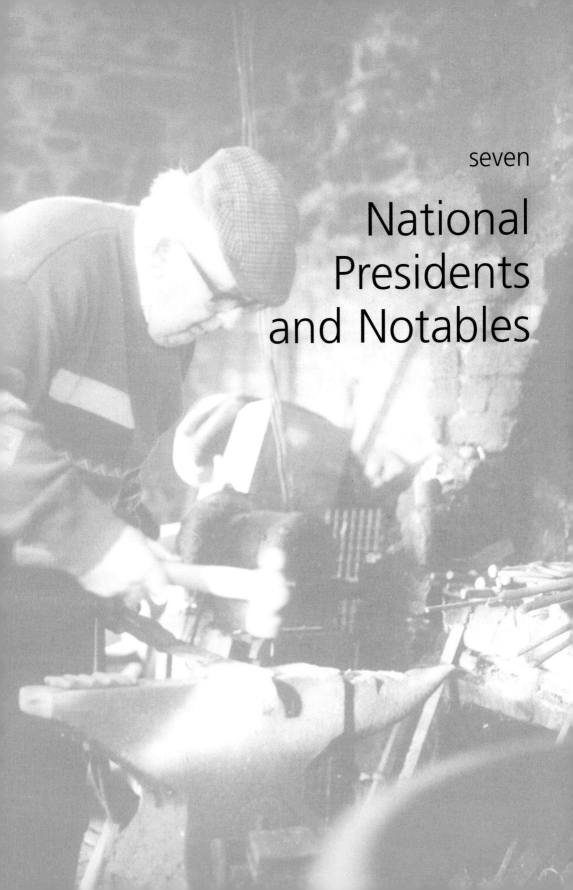

seven

National
Presidents
and Notables

*Above left:*Micheal Vincent (Vin) O'Donoghue was born in 1900. He qualified as an engineer and became a Volunteer with the Third West Cork Brigade. He took the republican side in the Civil War and later began to teach at Lismore CBS. After a fine hurling career he rose to be President of the GAA (Gaelic Athletic Association) in 1952. Vincent died in 1972. He is one of the six Lismoreians who went on to become presidents of national organisations.

Above right: Bobbie Begley is from Cooldelane, Lismore. After a fine athletics career he was elected to the executive of BLE (Bord Lúth-Cleas Éireann, the Athletics Board) and was Irish team manager in 1983 in Helsinki. Bobbie was created President of BLE in 1989. A fine communicator and extremely charismatic, Lismore is very proud of him. His commitment to athletics is near total.

Left: Tom Murphy was born in Lismore in 1906. Graduate B.Comm at UCC he became a teacher and taught most of his career at CBS North Brunswick Street Dublin. He was President of ASTI (Association of Secondary Teachers of Ireland) 1960–1961. Recognised as a fine teacher and an excellent astute leader, Tom retired in 1971 and died in 1972.

Above left: Mortimer ('Murty') G. Hynes was born in Lismore, in 1909, the son of Cyril Hynes. He graduated VS (Veterinary Surgeon) in 1934. He became a Veterinary Inspector in 1935 and Veterinary Director in 1964, retiring in 1974. A truly influential figure in the bovine and brucellosis eradication schemes, he organised the first maximum security quarantine station in Europe on Spike Island. He put farm advisory services on a new footing and was President of the AI (Artificial Insemination) Club and the Society of Animal Breeding of UK and Ireland.

Above right: John Barry was born in Glencairn, Lismore and was a founder member of the NFA (National Farmers' Association), later the IFA (Irish Farmers' Association). He rose up through the IFA and the Co-operative movement and served as President of ICOS (Irish Co-operative Society) 1982-1985 and a director 1976-1986. John was a great believer in what the co-operative movement could achieve, a true disciple of Horace Plunkett. A quiet but inspirational leader and lobbyist for farmers in Ireland and Europe, John died on the last day of 2002.

Right: Andy Coleman was born in Lismore in 1928 and became a pharmacist. Joining cow & Gate in 1960 he helped turn that company around in Ireland. Andy started his own pharmacy in 1970 which is now one of the busiest in Ireland. Andy J. was Vice-President of the IPU (Irish Pharmaceutical Union) 1976-1978. A man of rare intellectual ability Andy J. is still active and is too, a fine amateur archaeologist and antiquarian.

Jackie Ormonde was a heroic if un-trumpeted figure of the War of Independence, tunnelling his way out of Lismore Jail at 16 years. Taking the republican side in the Civil War he took a broad view of the new state saying, 'it needed to embrace all strands of opinion irrespective of background, and incorporate a right to foster its own culture, language, music and games'. A teacher turned Fianna Fáil politician, he was Minister for Posts and Telegraphs 1957-1959. An excellent hurler in his heyday, he was also a fine parliamentarian and orator. His son Donal also became a TD and daughter Ann a Senator.

Seán Goulding was Fianna Fáil TD for Waterford 1927-1937. He had a pub and hardware at the corner of Main street and Ferry Lane He was a great confidant of de Valera and a strong believer in bilingualism. In 1938, he became a member of Seanad Éireann and Chairman of that august House in 1943.

Right: Ollie Wilkinson TD and farmer is the current inheritor of the mantle of Seán Goulding and Jackie Ormonde. Elected in 2002, George Hennessy his dynamic agent said '-twas time to put a Wilkinson in the House sure he's the best that man can get!' A fierce worker on the ground his motto is, 'Ní neart go chur le chéile' (In unity there is strength: a salutary one for Lismore!). Ollie's surname exemplifies how intertwined Irish and British ancestry is: his family is the same branch as Johnny Wilkinson, England's recent rugby hero.

Right: Tim Healy, first Governor-General of Ireland. Tim spent his most formative years in Lismore where his father was Clerk of the Poor Law Union. He became an MP in the UK in 1880. Healy turned against Parnell over the O'Shea divorce case. A master of sarcastic invective he was known as 'Tiger' Tim. Governor General from 1922-1928 he died in 1931. A plaque to him in Lismore is on the wrong house; Tiger Tim is surely not amused!

Pádraig Ó Macháin (Patrick Vaughan) is a Professor in the School of Celtic Studies in Dublin. Born in 1960, he has many academic publications to his credit plus an account of Irish Manuscripts at Mount Melleray Abbey. He founded and edits *An Linn Bhuí, Iris Ghaeltacht na nDéise* and has edited the poems of Robert Weldon. Little wonder Pádraig is a writer and scholar with a father like Pad who wrote the popular monograph *The Last Forge in Lismore*.

Monsignor John Dean Kelleher was a native of Bishopstown, Lismore. A distinguished priest and scholar he was President of St John's College the Diocesan Seminary in Waterford but returned to pastoral duties in 1936. Seen in his early career as liberal and avant garde he was always a fine churchman and finally became Parish Priest of Ballybricken where building renewal consumed him. He lies buried in Ballybricken.

Fr John Michael O'Shea could rank with Marshall Ney as 'the bravest of the brave'. The Teaser, a Welsh schooner was wrecked in Ardmore Bay in 1911. Fr John took command of a boat and rescued the crew against great odds. His conspicuous courage and noble example became legendary. He received the RNLI gold medal, the silver medal of the Board of Trade, British Empire medal and George Cross. Another Lismoreian, Dan Lawton was in the rescue party also. Fr O'Shea died in 1942 as Parish Priest of Ballyporeen. Laura Whelan of Mayfield was his sister. His portrait hangs in St Declan's Hall in Ardmore to this day

Charles Geoffrey Nason Stanley 1884-1977, Dean of Lismore 1934-1961. Dean Stanley gave the oration at Dean William Beare's ordination, the present incumbent of Lismore Deanery.

Pad Vaughan at work in his forge. A doyen of iron with great durability. A brilliant artisan and fine hurler in his day, his monograph *The Last Forge in Lismore* is a real gem, indeed may become a classic of its genre.

Apart perhaps from Archbishop Robert Dunne, Tom Hickey is Lismore's most distinguished native son in the modern era. A brilliant graduate of economics at UCC, he became editor in London of the Statist, a famous economics journal founded by Tipperary man, Thomas Lloyd. Hickey practically invented the special supplements which had great influence in the Commonwealth. When the Statist folded it was reinvented as the Economist. Tom also co-founded the Irish Club in Eaton Square, London and became a well-known guest speaker. He met regularly with old Lismoreians in London down the years. He died in 1972.

Dr. O'Farrell MOH (Medical Officer of Health) from a snapshot in 1960. A grand old time medic, courteous and diligent: a credit to his high calling.

Jim Canning, Lismore's most romantic entrepreneur. Now entering pension-hood he lived a varied life always eyeing the main chance. His favourite sayings are: I bought that farm; never give a sucker a second chance.

George Heskin and Babs Canning. Two people who added to the gaiety of Lismore in featureless times. George farmed well but socialised better; he'd yarn till the cows came home and might not even notice they had gone back.

Lady of the dance, Órla Flynn. Órla is currently the head of the school of humanities at CIT (Cork Institute of technology). Born in New York Órla won the North American Championship in Irish Dancing at ten years of age, making her a champion of the world - the New World. The Flynns came home in 1977 and Órla proved a brilliant student at Lismore Convent and UCC. Órla captained UCC in some memorable camogie matches.

The focus in this photograph is on the man cutting the tape at a Boston Court House ceremony. He is Judge Al Burns recently retired. His great grandfather William Byrnes was born in Lismore in 1812. The O'Briens of Lismore-Cappoquin are also in the line. Byrnes was changed to Burns around 1850 in Canada. The Burns married into the Grainger family (originally Co. Kilkenny), one of whom became Chief of Police in Cambridge Mass, and two Graingers James and son Edmund who became famous Hollywood producers. The Sands of Iwo Jima starring John Wayne being a film of theirs. His family story stands for countless others from Lismore who achieved fulfilment abroad.

Left: Robert Boyle, 'Father of Modern Chemistry' 1627-1691. Born in Lismore, the fourteenth child of the Earl of Cork Richard Boyle, a blow-in who did well. Robert is famous for Boyle's Law which states that at constant temperature the volume of gas varies inversely with its pressure. He was too, effectively the founder of the Royal Society in 1663. A deeply religious man, Boyle had the bible translated into Irish and wrote theological treatises. We name him, 'The Greatest Lismoreian'

Left: Richard O'Farrell of Ballyanchor 1804-1883, was a tenant farmer and great grandfather of Brendan O'Farrell now in Ballyanchor and grandfather of the inimitable John O'Farrell undertaker of Midleton Co. Cork. Richard also collected rates for the Poor Law Union. He is buried in St Carthage's churchyard.

eight

Scenes around Lismore

This painting of the Spout was completed by Eddie O'Connor for project SMILE. The clearing away of greenery has exposed the Tower.

River Blackwater, Lismore, Co Waterford.

A panoramic view taken in the early twentieth century of the Blackwater from Lismore Castle. We can only wonder did the photographer step back in awe in trembling like James II back in 1689 on viewing the vista.

A reconstructed courthouse photographed on fair day June 1931. It had been burned down in 1920 in the liberation struggle. Note the modified belfry and absence, of a clock. Note too, the fair stall to right and men haggling over calf price to the left or is it the three-card trick man! The reconstruction was done by the Co. Council. Some men who worked on it were Tom Keating, Moss Willoughby, George O'Brien, Marsh Hickey (Regan), Bill Sheehan of Tallow and Paddy Nagle of Abbeyside. The granite steps came from Orpens House in Ballyduff.

The Funeral of Lord Cavendish, 1944. The good lord had died prematurely. He was held in high regard locally. Catholics turned out in numbers for his burial. We can see Jim 'Slog' Ahearne hands joined almost touching the wreath the man carries, also Jack Nugent to back and left of coffin and Matt Gough, Seán Doocey, John 'Jocklin' O'Donnell and Bill Landers all to left foreground.

St. Carthage's Church of Ireland in the North Mall. An antiquity of fourteen centuries though little of the original survives due to conflicts. A tower and spire were added to the building we saw earlier in the book in 1827. In 1830 a big bell was added which now rings the Angelus. The Mall or entrance avenue was opened in 1726. Lismore's most venerable antiquity it is endangered by heavy vehicles using the Mall as a turntable and parking lot.

Above: Fort William House Glencairn was built in 1836 for J.B. Gumbleton to the design of James & George Richard Pain who also designed Strancally Castle. A two-storey house of sandstone ashlar with a number of slight Tudor-Revival touches. The drawing room has a fine boiseries (wood carving) introduced by the second Duke of Westminster whose Irish home it was for a brief period in mid twentieth century.

Below: Glencairn abbey was built in 1619, acquiring its present name in 1800 when John Hogan built a new wing for Richard Gumbleton. It passed to Henry Bushe, then to the Powers and in 1932 to the Cistercian Sisters. A beautiful place to visit to contemplate much of the vanity and aimless striving that goes on outside the gates.

Above: Mount Melleray Abbey, founded 1832. The Cistercian monks came to Melleray at the request of Dr Fogarty Parish Priest of Lismore. Melleray became the symbol of resurgent Catholicism following the Catholic Relief Act of 1793; a symbol too perhaps that the penal laws were over.

Left: Brother Gerard hedge trimming in Melleray in 1975. Brother Gerard Leddy was from Araglen and a legendary figure in Melleray. The Prendergast's of Lismore have close ties with the Leddy's. A monk for nearly 80 years, Brother Gerard died in 1992 in his one hundredth year.

Strancally Castle is spectacularly sited on a bend in the Blackwater at Knockanore. Designed by James & George Richard Pain, who also designed Fort William House, for John Kiely-Ussher about 1830. It is close to the remains of an old Desmond castle notorious for its 'Murdering Hole', a hole in the rock through which the bodies of the lord's victims were cast into the river. The interior of the castle is rather plain: it has been sold and resold a lot in recent times.

An old image of the ice-house on the Ballyduff Road at Ballyin. Built around 1860 to store ice used for the preservation of salmon harvested from the Blackwater. The 'inches' were flooded by a water lock and left to ice up whence the ice was carted to the houses. There it was rammed into the chambers using a salt mixture to compound the ice. Ice-houses were in use up to the Second World War when refrigeration became popular. A spin-off pastime of iced-up inches in Lismore was ice-skating: Seán Goulding is said to be the first person to use skates in Lismore!

Castle Dodard (Dún Ard, High Fort/Haven) so called is more of a hunting lodge, built for Richard Boyle at Carrignagour. It fell into decay but Steve and Pam Stephenson acquired it from the Land Commission in 1969 and restored it. The current décor has an oriental flourish.

Dromana Gate or Moorish entrance to Dromana Estate on the river Finisk below Lismore. This Hindu-Gothic gate is modelled on Brighton pavilion and dates from around 1830. Built of wood to greet Henry Villiers-Stuart (the same Stuarts of the Lismore Nicotine factory) after his honeymoon it was later rebuilt in stone. An attractive gate lodge which is unique in Ireland.

Artistic impression of a restored Round Hill. Round Hill, a mile east of Lismore on the Blackwater, is a motte and bailey built by Prince John in 1185 as an outpost of the Castle. It became known as Lios Mór (The Big or Great Fort) alias Lismore.

Above: The Grand Lodges, Ballyduff Road, Lismore. Known also by other names such as the Towers and of course the Grand Follies. Built by landlord Kiely-Ussher in the nineteenth century. Against the odds they are today a major local tourist attraction so in a perverse way Kiely-Ussher has been vindicated as they were seen as a great extravagance in the days in which they were built.

A composite view of a restored Lismore Canal: artistic impression. The canal was completed towards the end of the eighteenth century, making Lismore a virtual inland port. It operated fitfully until about 1920. The canal has great potential as an amenity or boating, fishing, linear park and so on. Its restoration along with that of Round Hill is devoutly to be wished but worked towards.

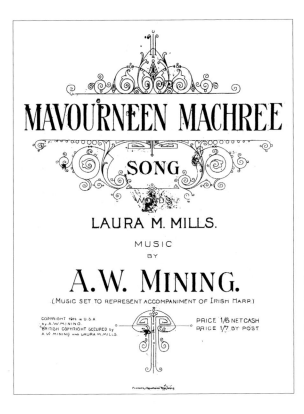

A Song by Laura Mills. The Mills lived where the Hornibrook's have their car business today. Laura was a poetess and songwriter. Her work tended towards the sentimental but what better way to end our photographic journey than with a song written by a local lady almost a century ago.

And so 'to the leaba' in a Irish Board Bed at Castle Dodard! This is a unique kind of bed-head affording protection from the leakiest roofs. What a fine Lismore invention! Codladh Sámh!

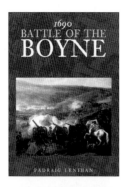

1690 Battle of the Boyne
DR PADRAIG LENIHAN

This book depicts the Battle of the Boyne: a battle that is commemorated every year and the largest battle in Irish history, it concluded the English war of succession, securing a Protestant monarchy in England.

0-7524-3304-0

A History of the Black Death in Ireland
MARIA KELLY

Maria Kelly goes in search of the 'Great Pestilence' whose consequences are often obscured by the intricate and tumultuous history of the time and traces how the Irish reacted to this seemingly invisible killer.

0-7524-3185-4

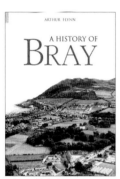

A History of Bray
ARTHUR FLYNN

This comprehensive volume recalls shops, businesses, churches, schools and some of the events that have occurred in the town. It also describes the lives of people who lived in the area over the centuries.

0-7524-3269-9

Dun Laoghaire-Rathdown
PAT WALSH

Dun Laoghaire–Rathdown sweeps from Dublin mountains to the sea and this collection of over 200 archive photographs shows the area's heritage, history and people at their best. The images provide a fascinating glimpse of life and the people of the area over the last century and more.

1-84588-500-7

If you are interested in purchasing other books published by Nonsuch, or in case you have difficulty finding any Nonsuch or Tempus books in your local bookshop, you can also place orders directly through our website
www.tempus-publishing.com